THE INVIOLABLE KINGDOM

John 4 and 18

Mystery, Majesty and Mathematics in John's Gospel #4

ANNE HAMILTON

The Inviolable Kingdom—John 4 and 18:
Mystery, Majesty and Mathematics in John's Gospel #4

© Anne Hamilton 2025
Published by Armour Books
P. O. Box 492, Corinda QLD 4075 Australia

Cover & interior design and typeset by Beckon Creative

Cover image composite: Lucky Girl Creative © 2020, Cottage Arts © 2019, Seatrout Scraps © 2017, Creative Memories © 2010, Forever Artisan 6 © 2024 courtesy of Forever.com;
DepositPhotos | sepavone, 'Tower of David in Jerusalem, Israel.'
Part 1: Lightstock | Kevin Carden 'Woman at the Well', Devon 'Jesus Baptism'; Unsplash | Yannis Papanastasopoulos; Zak's Jerusalem Gifts
Part 2: iStock | Ivan_off 'Baths for baptism among the pilgrims of the Orthodox confessions on the banks of the Jordan river. Israel'; CanStockPhoto
Part 3: Unsplash | Jared Subia, 'Crown'; Javardh, 'shallow-focus-photography-of-white-feather-dropping-in-persons-hand'; iStock | Nastco 'Feathers isolated on black background'; Creative Fabrica | Digital Curio
Part 4: Creative Fabrica | Topstar 'Spring Landscape Bridge with Flowers Art', Rose Art 'Vintage Medieval Scroll'
Part 5: Unsplash | Cristian Negraia 'Crown', Alex Noriega 'Crown of Thorns 0006'; iStock | tracielouise 'Young Lamb'; Dreamstime | Atm2023 'Model of Jerusalem city - in blue light'
Part 6: DepositPhotos | eunikas 'Roman ancient floor called lithostrotos - place where Pilate judged', fxquadro 'Proud Roman centurion warrior with plumed helmet'; Creative Fabrica | Rose Art 'Vintage Medieval Scroll'
Part 7: Lightstock | LUMO 'Jairus's Daughter', 'Pontius Pilate washes his hands' Creative Fabrica | pikepicture, AllisonSuns; Lucky Girl Creative © 2020

All other artwork: Beckon Creative

ISBN: 978-1-925380-82-8

 A catalogue record for this book is available from the National Library of Australia

All rights reserved. No part of this publication may be reproduced, stored in, or introduced into a retrieval system, or transmitted, in any form, or by any means (electronic, mechanical, photocopying, recording or otherwise) without the prior written permission of the publisher.

Note: Australian spelling and grammar conventions are used throughout this book.

The Inviolable Kingdom

ANNE HAMILTON

Unless otherwise noted, Scripture quotations are taken from The Holy Bible, Berean Study Bible, BSB Copyright ©2016 by Bible Hub Used by Permission. All Rights Reserved Worldwide.

Scripture quotations marked BLB are taken from the The Blue Letter Bible. Used by permission. blueletterbible.org

Scripture quotations marked BSB are taken from the The Holy Bible, Berean Study Bible, BSB Copyright ©2016 by Bible Hub Used by Permission. All Rights Reserved Worldwide.

Scripture quotations marked CEV are from the Contemporary English Version Copyright © 1991, 1992, 1995 by American Bible Society. Used by Permission.

Scripture quotations marked ESV are taken from the ESV® Bible (The Holy Bible, English Standard Version®), copyright © 2001 by Crossway, a publishing ministry of Good News Publishers. Used by permission. All rights reserved.

Scripture quotations marked GNT are from the Good News Translation in Today's English Version—Second Edition Copyright © 1992 by American Bible Society. Used by Permission.

Scripture quotations marked GWT are taken from GOD'S WORD®, a copyrighted work of God's Word to the Nations. Quotations are used by permission. Copyright 1995 by God's Word to the Nations. All rights reserved.

Scripture quotations marked ISV are taken from the Holy Bible: International Standard Version®. Copyright © 1996-forever by The ISV Foundation. ALL RIGHTS RESERVED INTERNATIONALLY. Used by permission.

Scripture quotations marked KJV are taken from the King James Version of the Bible. Public domain.

Scripture quotations marked NASB are taken from the New American Standard Bible®, Copyright © 1960, 1962, 1963, 1968, 1971, 1972, 1973, 1975, 1977, 1995 by The Lockman Foundation. Used by permission. (www.Lockman.org)

Scripture quotations designated NET are from the NET Bible® copyright ©1996-2016 by Biblical Studies Press, L.L.C. http://netbible.com Scripture quoted by permission. All rights reserved.

Scripture quotations marked NLT are taken from the Holy Bible, New Living Translation, copyright 1996, 2004. Used by permission of Tyndale House Publishers, Inc., Wheaton, Illinois 60189. All rights reserved.

Scripture quotations marked NIV are taken from the Holy Bible, New International Version®, NIV®. Copyright © 1973, 1978, 1984, 2011 by Biblica, Inc.™ Used by permission of Zondervan. All rights reserved worldwide. www.zondervan.com The "NIV" and "New International Version" are trademarks registered in the United States Patent and Trademark Office by Biblica, Inc.™.

Scripture quotations marked NKJV are taken from the New King James Version. Copyright © 1982 by Thomas Nelson, Inc. Used by permission. All rights reserved.

Scripture quotations marked NRS are taken from New Revised Standard Version of the Bible, copyright 1952 [2nd edition, 1971] by the Division of Christian Education of the National Council of the Churches of Christ in the United States of America. Used by permission. All rights reserved.

Thanks

Kevin and Jess, Judy, Kym, Hume,
Dorothy, Mark, Mark, Selwyn,
Will, Liz and John.

Table of Contents

Introduction	9
Part 1	14
1.1 Thematic Overview	17
1.1a Chiasmus	18
1.1b Recapitulation	21
1.1c Mantles	24
1.1d Water	29
1.1e Spiritual Powers	30
1.2 Focus on Women	33
1.3 Design Changes	37
1.4 A Kairos Node	39
1.5 A Well, A Stone, A Tree	44
1.6 Until Shiloh Comes	48
Part 2	52
2.1 Cleanness	55
2.2 Through Samaria	58
2.3 The Sixth Hour	61
2.4 Kingmakers	65
2.5 The Samaritans and Nabateans	68
Part 3	74
3.1 Give Me Sychar	77
3.2 Deflection	79
3.3 Primal Echoes	83
3.4 Living Water	86
3.5 The Well and the Pit	89
3.6 The Wife at the Well	92
3.7 The King's Cupbearer	97
3.8 Lord of the Covenant	100

Part 4 — 104

- 4.1 David Dancing — 107
- 4.2 Five — 117
- 4.3 Bridge-builders — 123
- 4.4 Call Your Husband — 131
- 4.5 Mastering Kingdoms — 135
- 4.6 Prophet You Are — 139
- 4.7 Tradition, Tradition — 146

Part 5 — 150

- 5.1 Pilate's Downfall — 153
- 5.2 Barabbas — 156
- 5.3 Salvation is from the Jews — 162
- 5.4 The Hour is Now — 164
- 5.5 In Spirit and Truth — 169
- 5.6 I Am — 172

Part 6 — 176

- 6.1 I See a Man — 179
- 6.2 The Barriers Fall — 182
- 6.3 The King Has Come — 185
- 6.4 The Harvest — 187
- 6.5 Thorns and Harvest — 193
- 6.6 The Covenant — 201
- 6.7 Symbols of Covenant — 208
- 6.8 I Cannot Tell — 211

Part 7 — 214

- 7.1 The Trap — 217
- 7.2 The Route and the Time — 219
- 7.3 Origins — 223
- 7.4 Prophets and Kings — 225
- 7.5 Prophets and Authorities — 229
- 7.6 Abijah — 238
- 7.7 The Seventh Hour and Beyond — 241
- 7.8 The Second Sign — 244
- 7.9 The Divine Right of Kings — 253
- 7.10 Conclusion — 259

Maps

- Route of Jesus, Jerusalem to Cana — 54
- Route of Jesus, Sychar to Cana — 220

INTRODUCTION

BACK IN THE FIRST DECADE of this century, I became interested in the structures of medieval poetry. The school where I was teaching was proposing to introduce an integrated curriculum, breaking down the barriers between compartmentalised subject areas. This required considerable research to establish the feasibility of combining mathematics, art, science and English. As a result, I stumbled across various works of scholarship into the arithmetical, geometrical and musical forms encoded in the lyrics, poems, jewellery and architecture of the Middle Ages.

I was so fascinated by what I read that I even began to correspond with some of the experts in the field. And I quickly found they were brilliant at analysis (much more than I was) but that I could do something they couldn't—I could *predict* what would appear on certain line numberings in particular poems. This talent amazed them. Some of them considered my ability a bit arcane when, ironically, that was the attitude most of their colleagues had about their research. But my knowledge wasn't esoteric. I had simply attributed THEOLOGICAL MEANING to the poetic structure, a risk so great in most academic circles these scholars would have been jeopardising their reputations to do so.

Yet it was unthinkable, in my view, for anyone living prior to our postmodern era with its deconstructionist ideologies to have produced 'mathematics for mathematics' sake'. This notion, similar to the notion of 'art for art's sake' where both form and symbols are emptied of meaning, is peculiar to contemporary culture. A fourteenth century poet, musician or designer just didn't think that way. They didn't divest their creations of sense; instead they invested them with interwoven layers of meaning.

It was also unthinkable, in my view, for anyone writing during the medieval period in the west to have *not* looked to Scripture for a pattern. The queen of subjects for these artists and artisans was theology—uniting and presiding over arithmetic, geometry, music, astronomy, grammar, rhetoric and logic. Thus, 490 surely meant *seventy times seven* and symbolised *forgiveness*. 153, likewise, would then refer to *resurrection* since it is mentioned in the scene where the apostles go fishing after Jesus is raised from the dead. 101 was somewhat trickier to decode, until I realised the philosophic connection between the Music of the Spheres and *God's sustaining power*.

Now I make this point about adopting a deconstructionist view, either consciously or unconsciously, because I believe that the form of John's gospel—the mirror-like literary design with its highly sophisticated numerical underlay—is likewise brimming with THEOLOGICAL MEANING. I don't think I should have to defend this position because it's so obviously obvious to me that this was the worldview of the writer. But, today, interpreting from an author's viewpoint has become a retrogressive way to look at literature, hence this introduction is fair warning. For me, the chiastic structure of John's gospel is elegant and artistic with an extraordinary architectural symmetry, but it's not primarily about a beautiful style that harks back to prophetic poetry. Many doublets, when linked together, form an information package, chockfull of unexpected secrets.

When I started this series, I had no expectation or pre-suppositions about what I'd find or even *if* I'd find anything beyond some nifty match-ups of names. I'm interested in the relationship between names and the callings over people's lives and I'd hoped for some deeper insight into that. However, as I've put the two halves of various chiastic elements together, I began to realise there were mysteries to be unveiled. There were so many references to Archimedes, for a start. Some were overt and some were subtle, but still, who'd have suspected that such a conflict even existed? Pythagoras, yes, I was ready for that, because Pythagorean theurgy is so prevalent in Gnosticism—to which John was so vehemently opposed. But Archimedes? He seemed to spring out of nowhere.

However startling as that was, an even more astonishing aspect revealed itself through the linking of the chiastic parallels. One by one, references to mantles began to tumble out of the text—and, along with them, the name of the disciple who had inherited a specific legacy through the agency of Jesus. First, Elijah's mantle was divulged. Then Joseph's.

Would there be a third? Moses soon came to light.

I started to look for them by the time that third one had appeared and quickly realised I'd failed to notice Reuben's. Not to mention Jacob's. Are there more? Of course! Are there seven? I'm not sure.

Still, once the pattern for discerning them became apparent, it was simpler to recognise the others as they emerged. And so, moving on to the fourth chapter, we are about to learn what happened to David's mantle. It should not surprise us that this is far from a straightforward matter, since David's mantle was torn apart when his grandson came to power, and the once-unified kingdom was divided into the territories of Judah and Ephraim.[1] There are

---

1   More commonly called the Kingdom of Judah and the Kingdom of Israel, or alternatively, the Southern Kingdom and the Northern Kingdom.

two pericopes in the fourth chapter—one about a Samaritan woman and one about a royal official whose son is ill—and in each are echoes of that savage sundering of a single monarchy into two thrones.

But Jesus, as usual, has come to heal history—to pass on a royal mantle to those willing to answer its call.

1.1 Thematic Overview

By the end of John's fourth chapter, we're 166 verses into the text. Working backwards from the final verse of the last chapter, there are 111 verses that match up with the ideas and elements in those 166 verses at the front.[2] Some parallelisms are thematically overt, such as:

> 'After this, He went down to Capernaum with His mother and brothers and His disciples'
>
> John 2:12[BSB]

complemented by:

> 'Then the disciples returned to their homes.'
>
> John 20:10[BSB]

Other pair-ups are exceedingly subtle, like the correspondence between the 153 fish and John the Baptist being unworthy to untie Jesus' sandals, or the correlation between the soldiers gambling for Jesus' clothes and the verdict of the Light. But, at least in every case so far, I've managed to find a profound connection. I'm not entirely sure at times I've found *the* allusion John actually intended to point to—I suspect I've sometimes missed the obvious, having caught a sideways glint of the unobtrusive.

Now, in addition to the chiastic aspects, John also focussed his attention on several other significant themes. He structured these all the way through the text, both forward and backward, right up to the end of the fourth chapter and beyond it. Built into his story record—and, in general, layered below the surface narrative—are multiple channels of weighty theological concepts. The repeated emphasis on these concepts shows how momentous they are in John's understanding of Christ's work on earth:

- Recapitulation
- Mantles and the passing on of inheritance
- Water—both of the earth and of the heavens
- Engagements with and against spiritual powers

These ideas have already been described in depth in the previous books in this series, so I will only briefly summarise them here. I will however include fresh material that has come to light since the last volume.

1.1a CHIASMUS

CHIASMUS IS A RHETORICAL AND LITERARY device that involves a repetition of thoughts or ideas in a reflected, mirror-like fashion.[3]

---

2 Verse numbering was only added to Scripture in the sixteenth century, so to expect a perfect verse-for-verse match of chiastic elements is unreasonable. Nevertheless, as has been noted in *The Elijah Tapestry* through *The Summoning of Time* and into *The Lustral Waters*, the correspondence of ideas, ranging through superficial to intensely profound, is in a stunning alignment.

3 Wikipedia distinguishes between 'chiasmus' and 'antimetabole', chiasmus having a reversal of grammatical structure but no repetition of words, while antimetabole has word repetition as well. Scriptural analysis of inverted grammatical clauses does not tend to such a hard and fast distinction. See: en.wikipedia.org/wiki/Chiasmus (accessed 18 September 2024)

John's entire gospel is structured this way, starting with a triple mention of the Logos in the first verse and ending with three references to *writing* in the last two verses.

Many fine examples of chiasmus, both from Scripture and elsewhere, are quoted in the previous books in this series. However I want to draw to your attention a small instance of the form in John's fourth chapter. My phrasing below is a little awkward, but it is close as possible to the Greek order, so as to show the reversed parallelism more clearly.[4]

   A   ...true **worshippers will worship** the Father

      B   IN THE SPIRIT AND IN TRUTH.

         C The Father seeks such to **worship** Him. God is SPIRIT,

      B' and IN THE SPIRIT AND IN TRUTH,

   A' those **worshippers must worship**.

John 4:23–24

This 'crossover' format[5] was often utilised by the prophets and was a notable feature of Hebrew poetry. John's gospel is therefore an epic poem in an ancient prophetic style. Although it has many aspects that conform to the ideals of Greek literature, it is conceptually Hebrew in design.

Peter Ellis[6] has built on the work of John Gerhard in analysing the gospel as a set of chiastic inclusions, rather than as a chronological

---

4   Emphases added to highlight different chiastic features.

5   The name 'chiasmus' or 'chiasm' was inspired by the Greek capital letter *chi*, X, with its two crossover strokes.

6   Peter F Ellis, *The Genius of John: A Composition-Critical Commentary on the Fourth Gospel*, Liturgical Press, 1984. John Gerhard, *The Literary Unity and Compositional Methods of the Gospel of John*, unpublished dissertation 1975. By 'inclusion', Ellis means a sequence that begins and ends with the same words and shows an internal chiastic structure.

narrative. The seeming disorder of the storyline compared to the synoptic gospels is therefore explained by the constraints of the poetic form.

Kym Smith has discerned that the gospel is constructed of 70 micro-chiastic pericopes[7]—that is, episodes that are mirror-reflective in their own right. There are also macro-chiastic structures that are symmetrical across several chapters. My belief goes further than any of these writers: the entire gospel is globally chiastic in nature.

Smith further notes the controversial possibility that the placement of the micro-chiastic elements in relation to the macro-chiastic elements forms a shape like a 'body' with outstretched arms. Contentious as this suggestion may be today, it would certainly not have been so in the past. Those medieval poets I mentioned previously would have anticipated that just such a spiritually significant design would be incorporated into the text and govern its structure. For them this was a perfectly normal expectation. They were simply adhering to a historical belief that mathematics and poetry were a natural and indivisible unity. This notion was worldwide in its acceptance until it disappeared in the west during the sixteenth century. Today we might think it's a quirky, wacky idea—but that just shows us up as cultural despisers of the past.

Educated Greek citizens in ancient times simply would not have taken seriously any writing that did not conform to their canon of beauty and truth—and those ideals happened to be based around the proportions of the human body. John, therefore, by using the Body of Christ as the basis of his literary set-up both kept the expected form while, at the same time, completely shattering it. He'd given his readers fair warning this would be the case in his iconoclastic opening line. There he mentioned the LOGOS—the

---

7 Kym Smith, *The Amazing Structure of the Gospel of John*, 2005

pinnacle of numerical loveliness in the eyes of the Greeks—within a 17-word sentence. 17 was a number to be avoided at all costs as a philosophic abomination.

Now it's possible to think of the symmetry of the human body as the basis of John's chiastic design, extrapolating that notion to the Body of Christ. In my view, however, the chiasmus symbolises blood covenant when, to 'cut' the promises, an animal was sacrificed and the two halves laid out so that the walk of blood could be performed, proclaiming both blessing and curse.

1.1B RECAPITULATION

LIKE CHIASMUS, RECAPITULATION IS A CONCEPT—at least as far as the Greeks were concerned—from the art of rhetoric. A speech-maker would sum up, that is, *recapitulate* his remarks in his closing statement. So it was understood that God, as the ultimate Speech-maker, the Speaker whose words brought forth the universe and all in it, had made His summary statement in the LOGOS, Jesus of Nazareth.

Recapitulation is the oldest theory of the atonement. It was first used in the second century by Irenaeus, bishop of Lyon. By *recapitulation*, Irenaeus referred to Jesus writing Himself into the storyline of salvation history, beginning a chapter in the same way as in the past but making changes at pivotal points to ensure that previous tragedies did not repeat themselves. Instead, a new and blessed ending came to pass. Where Adam had been tempted in a garden and fell, bringing death into the world, Jesus resisted the temptation and instead brought life for mankind. He mended the primal wound of the world, and healed history.

In this series, I have extended the concept of recapitulation far beyond the atonement, at least insofar as when 'atonement' is limited to the Cross and Resurrection. Jesus didn't start healing history at the crucifixion, He started at Cana. His every action, as described by John, was to undo the pain of the past that affected the present. This brought Jesus into immediate conflict with the spiritual powers of the region—great numbers of them, including Dionysius the 'twice-born', Herakles-Melkart—'king of the city', Zeus the lightning-wielder, Baal-Hadad the 'cloud-rider', Mithras—'lord of the contract' and 'light of the world', Resheph—gatekeeper of the underworld, Myrrh of the perfumes, Neith the 'shroud-maker', Athena the 'wise', Artemis of Ephesus and Anat the dispossessor. The struggles against these fallen spiritual authorities were not one-time battles but full-on wars with multiple engagements.

Prominent amongst the foes of Jesus was Anat, the Canaanite goddess sometimes dubbed the 'Queen of Heaven', who revelled in bloodshed, slaughter and untrammelled carnage. He's about to engage in warfare with her again in Samaria—after all, His stop at Jacob's Well would take Him right into the vicinity of Joseph's tomb. It was Joseph who had originally brought the influence of Anat into Israelite history. The Pharaoh he served renamed him Zaphenath-Paneah. The first element in that name is, in my opinion, simply a dedication to Anat through her title, *Anat of Zaphon*. Joseph didn't resist her influence, but instead succumbed to her pressure to dispossess others.

It was no coincidence that, just as Joseph invented forced resettlement to break the ties of the Egyptians to their ancestral land,[8] that this was the very fate to befall the people of Samaria, the land of his descendants, at the hands of the Assyrians. We

---

8   Genesis 47:21. See: rabbisacks.org/covenant-conversation/mikketz/joseph-and-the-risks-of-power (accessed 27 September 2024)

reap what we sow.⁹ Sometimes, however, the time of the harvest is so long in the future we forget what we have planted—and, in many cases, we have absolutely no idea what spiritual payload we have inherited from our ancestors. But the day of justice eventually comes.

Even so, God's mercy is unfailing. Jesus came to bring the cycle of reaping to a halt, to repair, to *recapitulate*, the old stories. He is more than God's summary statement on the acts of history, He also is God's verdict. Although we readily see Adam's sin, we're more than likely to view Joseph as righteous, a mature hero of the faith without fault or blemish. However, we need to look to the world-mending of Jesus in order to discover whether our view of the matter is in accord with the 'verdict of the Light'.¹⁰

In John's opening chapters and their chiastic partners, it's revealed that Jesus is:

- the new Adam
- the new Noah
- the new Joseph
- the new Moses
- the new Jacob
- the new Israel
- the new Joshua
- the new Phinehas
- the new Samuel
- the new Elijah
- the new Elisha
- the new Jonah

---

9   Galatians 6:7
10 John 3:19

We often overlook what the Jewish people call 'tikkun olam', *the mending of the world*, as an aspect of the Good News. Yet Jesus spent so much of His time in bringing about the healing of history. It's easy to notice where He healed people, but it's not so simple to come to grips with the fact that some of these people represented the wounded landscape around them. The woman of Samaria is one of these embodiments of history, so too is the royal official whose story occurs immediately after hers.

In each of these episodes, we see echoes of the past—a similar beginning to an old tragedy—before the plotline changes and joy comes bounding in.

1.1c MANTLES

OF ALL THE THEMES THAT JOHN layered into his record, the most unexpected—at least for me—is Jesus gathering up and distributing mantles to His disciples. Elijah's, Joseph's, Moses' and Reuben's have all been discussed in previous volumes.

John goes way beyond any declaration of a general inheritance in Christ for all the children of God, although that too is evident in his last chapter. He's so specific. There's nothing universal about these legacies: Simon Peter was given Elijah's mantle, Mary Magdalene received Joseph's, Nicodemus was granted Moses', John himself was handed Reuben's. The purpose of such a gift was not, of course, for them to repeat the works of those who'd worn the mantle before them. Rather, it was given so that they could mend the mistakes of the past, as well as advance the unfinished assignment that the previous bearer had failed to complete. All mantles carry a responsibility of healing—both of people and of the land. As disciples of Jesus, we are called to recapitulate too—to step into and walk out the old, old stories as they repeat themselves in the cycle of sowing-and-reaping, while also bringing the power of Christ's atonement to bear in order to change the endings so that the glory of God is revealed in His redemption of all things.

Now in retrospect, since I've become familiar with what to look for regarding mantles, I've realised I overlooked all the clues regarding Jacob's. His is the gift and the legacy Nathanael received. Recognising this, I wondered what Jacob's biggest mistake was. Of course there were many blunders on his part that needed a touch of healing and restoration from the Lord, but I tend to think the most significant was his failure to tell his extended family about the God of his father, Isaac, and his grandfather, Abraham.

When he fled from his uncle Laban, taking his four wives, his daughter and his eleven sons, his beloved Rachel took Laban's 'teraphim', her father's household gods, the spirit-housing for her ancestors. Her trust for healing was evidently not in the God of her husband—the One who revealed Himself to Jacob at Bethel, standing at the top of a ladder stretching between heaven and earth on which angels were ascending and descending.

Jesus, on first meeting Nathanael, describes Himself as that Ladder. Moreover, He describes Nathanael in terms of two names that both originally belonged to the same person:

> *Behold, an Israelite indeed, in whom is no deceit!*
>
> John 1:47 NKJV

Deceiver is one of the meanings of the name, Jacob, while *Israel* is the name Jacob received after wrestling with the angel of God. Jesus has basically said, 'Here is Israel without Jacob.' Surely that makes Nathanael the perfect candidate to take up Jacob's mantle and to dismantle the unholy choices of Jacob's life.

Now, I'm assuming that Jacob's grand error—above all others—was in spending 22 years in Paddan-Aram and not telling his relatives about the God who'd promised to keep and protect him. Perhaps he didn't even tell his wives—if Rachel actually knew about the God who had appeared in a dream to her husband at Bethel, she nevertheless put more faith in the healing power of the 'teraphim' than in any deity atop a ladder with angels ascending and descending on it. To rectify this mistake, Nathanael would have had to have gone as a missionary to Paddan-Aram and demonstrated the healing power of Jesus.

And indeed, according to early church history, this is precisely what he did. We're apt to think, based on the Book of Acts, that Paul was the only apostle to the Gentiles in the first century. This, however, was far from the case. Nathanael joined up with his fellow-apostle, Jude Thaddeus, who had initiated the work in Edessa, the capital of the kingdom of Osroene[11] in the ancient territory of Paddan-Aram.

Edessa was less than fifty kilometres[12] from Harran, the waypoint on the journey from Ur of the Chaldees where Abraham's father had tarried for some years. Harran was the place of departure for Abraham, Sarah and Lot when they left their wider family to travel on to the Promised Land. Harran was also where Abraham's servant found a bride for his master's son, Isaac, on stopping his camel train by a well. A generation later, when Jacob had to flee home because he was fearful of the revenge his twin brother Esau was about to extract for the duplicitous theft of his birthright, that very same well is the probable location for Jacob's first meeting with Rachel, the beautiful daughter of his uncle Laban.

---

11 This was, in prior times, ancient Mesopotamian-Armenia. Today's Armenia is 600 km to the north-east

12 30 miles

Although Harran remained pagan for centuries, even after the evangelistic work of Jude and Nathanael, the country as a whole was nevertheless the first to declare itself a Christian kingdom in the late second or early third century.

A delightful healing-of-history story is told about Jude's entry into Edessa and his welcome there. Years prior to Jude's arrival, the king of Edessa had heard about a man in Judea who went about healing the sick, casting out demons and working miracles. The fame of Jesus had reached right back to the country where the tribal heads of the nation of Israel had been born nearly two millennia previously. In this immediate general locality the sons of Jacob—Reuben, Simeon, Levi, Judah, Dan, Issachar, Napthali, Zebulun, Asher, Gad and Joseph—as well as their sister Dinah, all grew up as children. Only Benjamin was born in the Promised Land, as his name, *son of the south*,[13] indicates.

Now in the first century, the king of Edessa had an incurable illness. Realising that Jesus might be the answer to his disorder, the king sent Him a message as follows:

> *Abgar Uchama the Toparch to Jesus, who has appeared as a gracious saviour in the region of Jerusalem—greeting. I have heard about you and the cures you perform without drugs or herbs. If report is true, you make the blind see again and the lame walk about; you cleanse lepers and expel unclean spirits and demons, cure those suffering from chronic and painful diseases and raise the dead.*
>
> *When I heard all this about you, I concluded that one of two things must be true—either you are God and came down from heaven to do these things, or you are God's Son doing them.*

---

13   It can also mean *son of the right hand*, since *south* and *right hand* were synonymous once a person was correctly oriented by facing east. The original meaning of 'orient' in fact was *to face east*.

> *Accordingly I am writing to beg you to come to me, whatever the inconvenience, and cure the disorder from which I suffer. I may add that I understand the Jews are treating you with contempt and desire to injure you: my city is very small, but highly esteemed, and adequate for both of us.*[14]

Aren't those last few words simply classic? This town, Abgar was saying, is big enough for the two of us. Reportedly, Jesus declined this invitation, sending a return message via the Toparch's courier Ananias:

> *Happy are you who believed in Me without having seen Me. For it is written of Me that those who have seen Me will not believe in Me, and those who have not seen will believe and live.*
>
> *As to your request that I should come to you, I must complete all that I was sent to do here, and on completing it must at once be taken up to the One who sent Me. When I have been taken up I will send one of My disciples to cure your disorder and bring life to you and those with you.*[15]

Now, shortly after Pentecost, Thomas apparently felt inspired to dispatch Jude Thaddeus off to Edessa, the town that, according to its disease-ridden ruler, was sufficient for a couple of kings. Jude's presence in the city soon became conspicuous by the wonders he performed. When word reached Abgar, he quickly surmised this was the disciple Jesus had promised to send.

Jude was therefore summoned to lay hands on him, and Abgar was instantly cured. The miracle was so astounding the entire court lined up to be healed as well.

---

14   Elva Schroeder, *Whatever Happened to the Twelve Apostles?*, Even Before Publishing, 2010

15   Elva Schroeder, *Whatever Happened to the Twelve Apostles?*, Even Before Publishing, 2010

Jude Thaddeus was eventually joined by Nathanael who had first ministered in Arabia—a nation then centred on the Nabataean capital, Petra. The Nabataean royal house had dynastic links to Edessa, so it was natural to progress there.

Eusebius, the early church historian, writing in the fourth century said that, from Jude's time up until his own day, 'the city of Edessa has been devoted to the name of Christ.'

1.1D WATER

WATER, WATER EVERYWHERE! WELL, MAYBE not *every*where. Nevertheless John, more than any other early Christian writer, brings up the topic of water repeatedly. Over half of all references to water in the New Testament are found in his gospel and in the Book of Revelation.

And that count doesn't include all those things that involve water without it being specifically mentioned—like rivers and lakes, fishing and baptism—and even enlightenment. William Barclay, in discussing Hebrews 6:4-8, points out that baptism came to be synonymous with enlightenment: 'The light of knowledge and joy and guidance breaks in upon a man with Christ. So entwined with this idea did Christianity become that *enlightenment* ('phōtismos') become a synonym for baptism, and *to be enlightened* ('phōtizesthai') became a synonym for *to be baptised.*'[16]

John's repeated references to *light* and to *enlightenment* are therefore nuanced with overtones of *water*. This intriguing

---

16   William Barclay, *The Letter to the Hebrews, The Daily Study Bible Revised Edition*, The St Andrews Press, Edinburgh, 1976

theological partnership mysteriously pops up again in an unexpected way in modern physics: there light is described in terms of waves, and electromagnetism in terms of currents—two images of the ocean. In a similar fashion, ancient Hebrew poetically links 'yom', *day*, with 'yam', *sea*—a highly unusual coupling since most languages tend to associate *day* with *sun*, not with *water*. This is not the only Hebrew word linking *light* and *water*: 'nahar', meaning *light* or *shining*, also means *flowing* or *stream*. The 'mayim hayyim', *living water*, that is so significant a theme throughout the fourth chapter of John's gospel has, in the natural, this flowing, streaming, lustrous nature. In the spiritual, *living water* is a reference to the Holy Spirit and thus to fire, wind and light.

Most name dictionaries define the meaning of John as *God is gracious*. However, as outlined in *The Lustral Waters*, there is an overlap with the name Jonah—a water-evoking name if ever there was one, despite its assigned meaning of *dove*. More significant still is the high level of entanglement with the name of the water-god worshipped in Nineveh: Oannes.

John's focus on water is, at least to my mind, a natural outcome of trying to disengage his own name from that of a foreign principality, and ensuring its dedication to Jesus, the one true and Living Water. It is, after all, only by entering through faith into the wound in Jesus' side that we can be born again in Water and the Spirit.

1.1E Spiritual Powers

In the last quarter of the twentieth century, many denominations began to look for translations that had removed patriarchal language from the Bible. In some cases this was warranted. For instance, the Greek word 'adelphos' refers to those *born from the same womb*, thus to *siblings* or *brothers and sisters*, not merely to *brothers*.

Strict accuracy is one thing, ideology is another. In addition to feminising God, many church congregations ditched the warfare references as well, deciding that they were a symptom of toxic masculinity. At the other end of the spectrum, some believers saw themselves as under spiritual attack and began to take up a position of authority in high-level warfare against principalities and territorial powers. Receiving retaliation, they came to expect it as part and parcel of the conflict.

Both stances are, in my view, extreme. The first turns a blind eye to the repeated battles of Jesus against both demonic foot-soldiers as well as fallen angelic generals. The second stance all too often ignores the guidelines of Scripture for spiritual warfare, in the naïve belief that 'all authority' means we can cast such restrictions aside.

John's gospel focuses on the cosmic commanders, those dark angelic majesties who are the godlings and goddesses of pagan nations. In particular, he has directed his attention to the Phoenician and Canaanite deities: Baal-Hadad, the storm-god and so-called 'Cloud-Rider', along with his sister Anat—a goddess of carnage and dispossession whose claims of superiority are so great she directly challenged Jesus in many spheres. She asserted she was the one who overcame Death and Judgment, and had the right to determine who should occupy the throne over all creation.

In John's fourth chapter, Anat is featured once again. This time her presence behind the scenes is even more understated than in previous chapters—though, having said that, I doubt if it was in any way subtle back in the first century. It's only because of the passage of two millennia that we're faced with an archaeological dig into the literary layers of the gospel. For every word-treasure we unearth, it's necessary to carefully brush off the dust of the ages and examine it to try to determine its purpose. Yet, as soon as John reveals that Jesus has gone to the locality that Jacob bequeathed to Joseph, the clues are already in place that this story is once again about inheritance and the issues of dispossession that developed out of Joseph's Egyptian identity as Zaphenath-Paneah, a name that I believe encodes multiple meanings including *Face of Anat of Zaphon*.

Mary Magdalene re-enacts so much of the legend and ritual of Anat in her search for the body of Jesus on the day of resurrection that it's no wonder she was the recipient of Joseph's mantle. Together with Jesus, she is a despoiler of Canaanite liturgy and she recapitulates, and thus reverses, the tragic error of Joseph in disinheriting the Egyptians and giving them no way to redeem their land or buy themselves back out of slavery. She is the antithesis of Zaphenath-Paneah, the *Face of Anat of Zaphon*.

Throughout John's gospel, Jesus shows us a range of strategies for spiritual warfare. It's easy to miss what He's doing because it doesn't look violent or aggressive. Some of His battles involve overt displays of divine power, while some of them are such ordinary, simple interactions that the spiritual conflict is hardly noticeable. We're about to examine just such an everyday dialogue that hides an extraordinary battle.

Much as some believers today want to write spiritual warfare out of the Scriptural picture, that's not really an option. Jesus shows us just how much it was part of the normal routine of life.

1.2 Focus on Women

IN THE FOURTH CENTURY THE early church historian, Jerome, famous for his translation of the Bible into Latin,[17] dedicated some of his writing to women. Amongst his patrons were devout, ascetic females who belonged to wealthy families connected with the senate and he honoured their support. This naturally drew considerable criticism.

He rebuffed the detractors: 'These people do not know that while Barak trembled, Deborah saved Israel, that Esther delivered from supreme peril the children of God… Is it not to women that our Lord appeared after His Resurrection? Yes, and the men could then blush for not having sought what the women had found.'[18]

---

17   Jerome's translation, commonly called the Vulgate, is often criticised for rendering the text freely instead of strictly and literally. However, in my view this assessment is not entirely fair. While reading David Howlett's *British Books in Biblical Style*, I realised Jerome had set himself an additional constraint on his translation that made his task heroically more difficult. Howlett, to demonstrate what he meant by 'Biblical Style' so he could apply the term to various early insular texts, began by analysing the mathematical underpinnings of the Hebrew *Masoretic* text, the Greek *Septuagint* and the Latin *Vulgate* for Genesis 1. It became clear through this process that, while the Septuagint translators had ignored the numerical layering of the Hebrew, Jerome had not. In rendering the text into Latin, he also tried to keep as much as possible of the original mathematical proportions.

18   See: christianitytoday.com/history/issues/issue-17/quick-quotes-on-women-in-early-church.html (accessed 2 August 2023)

Jerome might well have pointed out the ministry of Jesus Himself was supported by several well-to-do women.[19]

The sidelining of women is an old, old problem that goes back far beyond the earliest days of the church. Many people think it's a result of a patriarchal society in ancient times, but I personally doubt that. In the days of the patriarchs, women were still named, their deeds and songs recorded. True, they were part of the background but we nonetheless know more about various slave women and maidservants, midwives and widows than we do about tribal heads like Asher or Issachar, Napthali or Zebulun.

It was only as the era of the kings approached that women began to become invisible. The shift starts towards the end of the period of the Judges. Early on, we're told of Achsah, Deborah and Jael, as well as Ruth, Orpah and Naomi. Later, Delilah and Hannah come under a significant spotlight. However, in tandem with this, a transition into anonymity occurs with 'Jephthah's daughter', the 'Levite's concubine' and the woman who dropped the millstone on Abimelech.

Female names are vanishing, even if the actions of women are not. The exception is often the daughters or wives of royalty, but even then, that's not always the case. Of Solomon's seven hundred wives and three hundred concubines, we know only Naamah, the mother of Rehoboam. Although his marriage to Pharaoh's daughter is mentioned several times, we aren't given her name. Nor do we know the identity of Jeroboam's wife, despite a significant story involving her. And by 'significant', I mean it is a matter of such historical weight that Jesus has to address it in His work of mending the past. As we shall see, John relates the circumstances of that healing in his fourth chapter.

---

19   Luke 8:3

It wasn't the patriarchs who erased women,[20] but the kings. In desiring to make a name for themselves, they thrust others into the background—women, even more so than men. It was Jesus who began to give ordinary women back their names and their visibility: in the gospel accounts, we find the stories of Mary and Elizabeth; we learn of Joanna and Susanna, financiers to the ministry of Jesus; we hear of Salome and of Mary, the wife of Clopas. Paul was helped by various women, including Phoebe—whom he calls his *coach* or *mentor*.[21]

It's curious, then, given the prominence of women in John's gospel that, in his fourth chapter, he doesn't actually identify the Samaritan woman. Perhaps, after more than fifty years, he'd forgotten her name. Or perhaps not. After all, he doesn't identify the royal official featured at the end of the chapter, either. Nevertheless, sufficient clues exist to name the official and thereby deduce John remembered him. Now it's more than likely any similar hints regarding the name of the Samaritan woman have become completely impenetrable with the passage of time. However, that's not going to stop me examining a suggestion of James McGrath[22] that a Hebrew or Aramaic equivalent of the woman's traditional Greek name, Photini, might have much to commend it.

---

20   Seven women prophets are recognised in Judaism: Sarah, Miriam, Deborah, Hannah, Abigail, Huldah and Esther. Of these, four are before the era of the kings, two were royal wives, and only Huldah from the time of King Josiah is from a later period and not (apparently) related to royalty.

21   She was also a deacon, though many translations tend to obscure this, just as many translations tend to hide the fact the Proverbs 31 wife is a woman of *valour*, rather than of *virtue* or *noble character*. As soon as Scripture translators choose to make an exception for a word that describes a woman, rendering it in a way that is uniquely different from that which commonly describes a man, theology is given precedence over God's word.

22   James F McGrath, *What Jesus Learned from Women*, Cascade Books, Oregon, 2021

Yet, why would John conceal these names? Perhaps it was to protect the remaining members of their families. However, that wouldn't have worked particularly well for the royal official since he'd been outed in Luke's gospel anyway.

Alternatively, as I've come to suspect, perhaps John was laying a trap for the Gnostics. After all, his gospel was written to oppose that heresy and, while the movement was a very diverse one, common to all its branches was a belief in salvation through secret, esoteric knowledge. But—and perhaps this was John's challenge to them—what was such knowledge worth if you couldn't do something as simple as identify the 'Samaritan woman' or the 'royal official'? He may have been baiting a trap to expose the conceit that the Gnostic adherents were an elite, privy to divine inspiration and salvific knowledge that lesser mortals didn't share. In conjunction with this, it is possible the names were secret as an early example of the 'disciplina arcani', *instruction in the mysteries*, a church custom wherein knowledge of particular doctrines and rites was withheld from the uninitiated so that they would not fall into simplistic heresy because of their lack of education in the faith.[23]

It was the kings, not the patriarchs, who rubbed out women's identities and vocations. Only when Jesus came as the King of kings were their names visible again, along with their roles. We may not be sure of the identity of the woman of Samaria but we can be sure of the momentous office Jesus entrusted her with: He appointed her as His first evangelist.

---

23   See: ccel.org/ccel/schaff/encyc01/encyc01.html?term=Arcani%20Disciplina (accessed 20 January 2025)

1.3 Design Changes

Up to this point in his narrative, John's chiastic matches have been ones of fine and precise detail along with occasional swirls within the episodes he was recording. Now, however, we come to the longest conversation that Jesus has with anyone in any of the gospels. There's a long discourse later in John, covering five chapters, but it's not a dialogue like this exchange between Jesus and the woman of Samaria. Their interaction is longer than that of Jesus with Nicodemus in the previous chapter and longer still than its chiastic partner, the interrogation before Pontius Pilate.

Consequently, the parallels have become very much broad brushstroke rather than the exquisitely polished matches we've seen previously. Now we have to consider whole blocks rather than single verses. The fine tuning of strict inverted parallelism has gone, though general correspondence remains. This is to be expected when swathes of dialogue are being reported. It would be beyond credible that the discussion between Jesus and the Samaritan woman exactly and inversely matched the question-and-answer session with Pilate.

Yet there are fitting pairs of thought across both conversations. Clearly these pairs are the reason John selected a story overlooked by all the other evangelists to mirror with the trial of Jesus. Underlying the meeting between Jesus and the Samaritan woman are the same themes as occur in the judgment before Pilate.

However, John has more in play than simple chiasmus. His thematic links between adjacent episodes are becoming deeper as are the connections through the chiasmus to a flanking scene. In addition, John has not left off recording the dispensation of mantles by Jesus to His followers. The woman of Samaria, Jesus' first evangelist, receives half of a mantle. The other half is given to the royal official who comes to Jesus, pleading for the healing of his son. That story is, naturally, told in the very next pericope.

A mysterious ethnic relationship exists between the woman and the official—at least, I believe there's one, assuming I have correctly identified him and haven't misread the clues. That relationship raises a host of uncomfortable questions. We are conditioned to read the Hebrew Scriptures in the light of the values esteemed by our culture. We are not taught to read the biblical record through the eyes of God, as shown in the way Jesus heals history.

Throughout the previous books in this series, I've emphasised the statement of Jesus: *No one is good, except God alone.*

Unfortunately we've been schooled to think of villains in Scripture in contrast to faith heroes who are held up for us to emulate. Yet everyone is a complex mixture of light and dark.

1.4 A Kairos Node

In *The Summoning of Time*, I pointed out that our current Christian notion of 'Kairos time' is a heavily sanitised version of what was originally a very violent concept. Kairos was not simply a favourable hour or a matter of seizing the day and making full use of the opportunities life presents us, it was the instant to strike when others were vulnerable. The earliest notions of the winged godling Kairos have overtones of ritual sacrifice.

In Pythagorean mysticism, Kairos involved a linkage of the perfect time and place—a knot or node in space-time where circumstances were flawlessly aligned, everything 'fit' together precisely and the moment to 'strike' was now. Ultimately, over many centuries, Kairos came to be understood as a mirror of cosmic perfection, reigning over measure, harmony and equilibrium.

Jesus creates such a sublime and ideal node when He journeyed to Sychar. As before, He picked up frayed and broken threads from the past and repaired them. In *The Summoning of Time*, it was shown how He healed history at Cana, mending the great wounds of dispossession that had been wrought through:

- Noah cursing Canaan
- Joseph exchanging land for food during the famine in Egypt, breaking the people's ancestral ties to their inheritance by forced resettlement and failing to provide them with any way out of slavery

Jesus isn't finished with Joseph. There's still healing to bring to that story. So He's come to the locality where Joseph is buried. But it's also the place where the first king *in* Israel, though not *of* Israel, was crowned. It's the place where the grandson of David witnessed the kingdom torn asunder through his own prideful foolishness. Sychar isn't just the place where Jacob dug a well, it's a place of blessing and cursing, of sworn fealty and of treacherous disloyalty, of covenant-raising and reaffirmation. It's the ideal place for the Samaritans to declare allegiance to Jesus as the Messiah.

- It was here that Abraham built the first of seven altars in the land God promised to his descendants.
- It was here that Jacob finally committed himself to the God of his fathers by burying his household idols under a tree. Probably the same tree where his grandfather had built that altar. Jacob also built an altar to *El Elohe Israel*.
- It was here that Joseph was buried on the plot of land given to him as a legacy[24] by his father. His bones were carried through the wilderness for forty years during the desert wanderings by the Israelites. They were finally laid to rest as he'd instructed in the ground he'd

---

24 Jacob buys the land (Genesis 33:19), though curiously he states he took it from the Amorites with his sword and his bow (Genesis 48:22), and it is here Joseph wants his bones to rest. Likewise, Abraham bought a cave in Hebron to use as a burial plot. Presumably Sheerah, when she built the cities of Upper and Lower Beth Horon as well as Uzzen Sheerah, also bought the land they were built on.

been promised centuries previously as a covenantal inheritance that passed down from his great-grandfather through his father.

- It was here that Joshua carried out the instruction of Moses to go and reaffirm covenant with God as soon as possible after entry into the Promised Land. Later, at the end of his life, Joshua set up a stone pillar as a witness and encouraged the people to reaffirm covenant once more. That stone was probably under the tree where Abraham had built that first altar and Jacob had buried his household idols, right next to the well he'd dug.

- It was here that Abimelech, Gideon's son, was proclaimed king—the first king of a tribe of Israel. It happened under the great tree by a pillar, so once again it seems the weight of all the sacred and historical associations that went back as far as Abraham were utilised to bring solemnity to the occasion. Abimelech had been given money by the local citizens from the temple of Baal-Berith and he'd used it to hire scoundrels to help him kill his seventy brothers. Just one, Jotham, escaped alive. Baal-Berith, *lord of the covenant*, is a natural deity for the area given all those covenant reaffirmations that had occurred in the past.

- It was here that Rehoboam, grandson of David, came for his coronation. Instead of winning the hearts of the people, he provoked them to rebellion by declaring he'd be an even harsher taskmaster than his father Solomon. The burden on the populace was already so taxing and intolerable that Solomon was described with the very same words as those used for the Pharaoh who'd enslaved the Israelites back in the days of Moses. The Tabernacle had been created from freewill offerings, voluntary effort and Spirit-endowed creativity; the Temple was built by forced labour, foreign expertise and deliberate underpayment.

Why Rehoboam did not choose the magnificent environs of the Jerusalem Temple for the coronation ceremony is unclear. But it was at Shechem[25] he made his ill-advised declaration that he would increase the load on the people and scourge them with scorpions, not mere whips. His statement incited a revolt that divided the kingdom. Ten tribes followed the rebel leader Jeroboam and only Judah still remained to Rehoboam. The Levites, scattered in many towns throughout the land, apparently followed local leadership.[26]

Seven different men had been involved in covenantal actions, involving both the swearing of fealty and the taking up of an inheritance. They'd all chosen the same place—right at Jacob's well or its immediate vicinity—as the site for their special event. Five of the seven either honoured God by pledging loyalty to Him or else were honoured by the loyalty of their compatriots. The last two destroyed relationship with the wider community before it even began. Rehoboam conceded to Jeroboam who became the first ruler of the northern kingdom. As the record in the Book of Kings put it:

> 'So Israel has been in rebellion against the house of David to this day.'
>
> 1 Kings 12:19[NIV]

---

25 Sychar, now the locality of Askar, was at the foot of Mount Ebal. It was about a kilometre north of Jacob's Well and in the direction of Mount Gerizim. The ruins of ancient Shechem were at Sychar. Jesus stopped just short of the place where Rehoboam lost the kingdom. Perhaps, as the Son of David, He was waiting for an invitation to return and a welcome for the heir of the kingdom.

26 The tribe of Benjamin eventually allied itself with Judah, and the Levites increasingly migrated to Jerusalem.

It's that millennium-old rebellion Jesus came to resolve in this Kairos moment. The woman of Samaria, as He will reveal, has had five husbands and is involved in a sixth relationship that reflects, in her own rebellion against convention, the old revolt against the line of David. So she perfectly represents the history of the landscape that needs both healing and restoration of inheritance—just as much as she does.

1.5 A Well, a Stone, a Tree

JOSEPH, ELEVENTH SON OF JACOB, was in prison in Egypt when he was suddenly sent for to interpret Pharaoh's nightmarish dream. Correctly explaining its meaning, he was elevated to the rank of viceroy, second-in-command only to Pharaoh himself. He was given the name Zaphenath-Paneah—in my view constituting not just a name covenant with Pharaoh but also indicating a dedication to the Canaanite war goddess who was the Pharaoh's own patron.[27] Joseph, in being known as the *Face of Anat of Zaphon*, was the conduit through which Anat was the influencer who nudged Joseph into completely dispossessing the Egyptians of their inheritance. In the third year of the famine, when ordinary farmers had no money left and no cattle either since they'd bartered their livestock for food in the second year, they sold themselves into slavery and gave over their land. Joseph accepted the offer, but gave them no way out. He did not set any year of Jubilee when the land would return to its former owners and all inheritance would be restored, but instead he broke the people's ties to their ancestral land by forced resettlement. Then

---

27 A seven-year famine occurs in the Canaanite legend of Anat and her brother Baal-Hadad. When Joseph interpreted the dream as pertaining to such an upcoming event, Pharaoh would no doubt have been reminded of the sacred writings of his patron goddess. He would naturally conclude she had sent Joseph as her ambassador to interpret the dreams and thus it would be appropriate to rename Joseph for her and marry him off to a woman named Asenath, *sacred to Anat*. See: *The Summoning of Time*.

he gave the best of the pastureland to his brothers and their families. He established permanent famine measures, giving back to the people the very grain they'd paid in taxes in exchange for their family's inheritance. The political mechanism he put in place would, in time, would be used against the Israelites by a later Pharaoh.

Joseph of course didn't want this policy to apply to himself. He wanted to inherit land and he wanted to be buried on that home plot. And so, because of the inexorable sowing-and-reaping principle built into the very fabric of the universe, his descendants were subjected to the same kind of forced resettlement programme as he'd invented. The Assyrians deported the people of the land, sending them out into the nations and bringing in, as their replacements, citizens from other countries. There were five major centres where the immigrants were transferred from, as they were forced to resettle in a new land.

As noted in *The Summoning of Time*, Jesus began His ministry by declaring war on Anat, the spirit of dispossession who claims to govern the appointed times in our lives. He didn't do so openly, of course—at least not from our perspective twenty centuries on. But it would have been quite obvious to those who knew the countryside back in the first century.

In this encounter with the Samaritan woman, we see yet another brief skirmish with Anat. This, of course, would have been a natural and opportune time to do so since Joseph's tomb is nearby. He addresses the woman as 'Woman,' which as noted in *The Summoning of Time* is 'anath' in Aramaic, and that happens to be the Greek name for Anat.

Moreover, He's come to a sacred well, a holy tree, a stone of witness. Here we have the subtlest of evocations of both Baal and Anat. In Canaanite liturgy, Baal offers to reveal to his sister Anat, in the sanctuary of Zaphon, the secret word of creative power through tree and stone. Baal, high and lofty and set apart from humanity, is said to understand the word of tree and the whisper of stone, the murmur of the heavens to the earth, and the sighing speech of the seas to the stars.[28]

While there is no direct evidence that Anat was worshipped at Shechem, it is however known that, according to a text from the ancient city of Ebla, Resheph was the city's patron-god.[29] Resheph, the gatekeeper of the underworld in Canaanite mythology, was frequently worshipped along with Anat and was associated with healing, pestilence and war. He was symbolised as a stag.

Despite the lack of direct archaeological or textual evidence for the worship of Anat at Shechem, it's my view that the gospel itself suggests it. A contest between Jesus and Anat plays out here because she is the goddess who claimed to be the kingmaker amongst the gods—the one with the right to choose who should rule.[30]

Shechem wasn't simply the seat of the first government for the tribal confederation, the very sense of its name was evocative of government. Shechem means *shoulder* or *ridge*. For the Israelites of old, a shoulder was a symbol of rulership and administration because, when someone wanted to confer high office on another, a set of keys would be placed on his shoulder. Hence the messianic prophecy:

---

28 See: jewishphilosophyplace.com/2015/07/07/baal-understands-the-word-of-the-tree-the-whisper-of-stone-stories-from-ancient-canaan/ (accessed 1 November 2024)

29 See: ldsscriptureteachings.org/2018/02/resheph-god-of-war-pestilence-and-the-underworld-in-the-hebrew-bible/ (accessed 1 November 2024)

30 See: Gregorio del Olmo Lete, Jordi Vidal and Nicolas Wyatt (eds.) *The Perfumes of Seven Tamarisks: Studies in Honour of Wilfred G. E. Watson*, Ugarit-Verlag, Münster 2012 — 'And may Anat the power<ful> drink, the Mistress of Kingship, the Mistress of Dominion, the Mistress of the High Heavens, [the Mistre]ss of the Earth.'

> *For unto us a child is born, unto us a son is given: and the government shall be upon His shoulder: and His name shall be called Wonderful, Counsellor, the mighty God, the everlasting Father, the Prince of Peace.*
>
> Isaiah 9:6 KJV

Jesus' words at Sychar are imbued throughout with kingship and governmental overtones. It's as the Prince of Peace that His contest with Baal-Hadad—Anat's favourite brother and her choice for the throne of the high king of all gods and nations—begins to heat up.

In Canaanite ritual, Baal sends this despatch to Anat after his victory over the Sea:

> 'Message of Baal the Conqueror, word of the Conqueror of Warriors:
>
> Remove war from the earth, set love in the ground, pour peace into the heart of the land, tranquillity into the heart of the fields.'

Sounds like something we'd expect Jesus to say, doesn't it? Yet, to the contrary, He said there will always be wars and rumours of wars. And although He commands us to love one another, He had to come to die to make that possible. True sacrificial love is not a matter of willpower or prophetic decree. It can only come about through the power of His atonement applied to our lives.

Baal, the so-called Cloud-rider, was Anat's choice for the kingship of heaven. The sustained battles against the two of them described in John's gospel indicate that they were enemies Jesus did not take for granted.

Peace does not come through the agency of Baal but from Jesus, the Prince of Peace.

1.6 Until Shiloh Comes

THERE ARE FOURTEEN DIFFERENT PLACES in the world called 'New York'. Of course most of the time we don't attach any geographical tags to the name because it's assumed we mean New York City in New York state on the eastern seaboard of the United States. However, there are six other New Yorks in the USA alone, so we'd need to clarify the location if we wanted to talk about another one: New York, Kentucky, for instance, or New York, Texas.

When a great many specific geographical pointers are given in Scripture about a location, a logical reason for the wealth of detail is to distinguish it from another place of the same name that is much more well-known. Consider:

> *There is the annual festival of the Lord in Shiloh, which lies north of Bethel, east of the road that goes from Bethel to Shechem, and south of Lebonah.*
>
> Judges 21:19[NIV]

This specifies a locality now known as Khirbet Seilun, where a tower has been built and a heritage display erected. However, despite extensive archaeological digs in the area, no evidence of a Tabernacle complex has ever been found.³¹ Although it's clearly the spot so carefully described in the Book of Judges where an annual festival and dance took place, it is nonetheless probably *not* the site of the Tabernacle.

The Septuagint, the Greek translation of the Hebrew Scriptures that was completed several centuries before Christ's birth, places the reaffirmation of covenant led by Joshua at Shiloh, not Shechem.³² In the valley of Shechem, there still exists a locality known as Ta'anath Shiloh, *approach to Shiloh* or *opportune sanctuary*. That meaning *opportune* should rightly remind us of Anat whose name is found encoded in Ta'anath Shiloh.

More importantly, over two millennia ago, when the memory of ancient days was much closer to the original source, Shiloh was pinpointed as the place within the Shechem region where Joshua placed the stone of witness and held a covenant ceremony. That also suggests Shiloh is the place where Abraham built his altar, Jacob buried his idols and dug his well, and Joseph's tomb was located.

---

31 It's pointed out that, since the Tabernacle was housed in a tent, then it's not surprising no archaeological evidence is forthcoming. This seems to be a rationalisation, however, since Gilgal, for instance, which was only used for fourteen years has left a mark on the landscape. (See: israelhayom.co.il/article/117681 —accessed 2 November 2024) According to the Jewish Board of Deputies, the Tabernacle was located first at Gilgal, then at Shiloh for 369 years before it was moved to Nob and Gibeon. (See: ijs.org.au/synagogue-services/ —accessed 19 February 2024) No mention is made by the Board about Shechem or Mizpah, perhaps reinforcing the idea that Shechem and Shiloh can be co-identified as the same. Mizpah, since it probably means *muster for war* or *gathering place for battle*, may well have been a moveable location and might also be, at least at times, identical to Shechem. It's therefore my view that, in 369 years, there should be *some* archaeological evidence at Khirbet Seilun if it is indeed the original site of the Tabernacle.

32 See: academia.edu/41723005/ (accessed 1 November 2024)

It makes sense that Shiloh in Shechem (Ta'anath Shiloh), rather than Shiloh near Bethel (Khirbet Seilun) is the seat of the first government in Israel, the place where the Tabernacle was set up, the land was divided, and from where priests like Eli and judges like Samuel ruled. Ta'anath Shiloh has the weight of association with several revered patriarchs aligned with it, while Khirbet Seilun, 17 kilometres to its south-west, has none.

So if this identification is correct and Jesus, in coming to Sychar, also came to Shiloh, then He visited the ancient sanctuary where Hannah prayed so desperately for a child. He came to the place where the boy Samuel had his visions of God, to the shrine that had been defiled by Eli's sons and gradually abandoned after the loss of the Ark of the Covenant and the fall of the house of Eli.

The Ark finally returned in the Person of Jesus.

But there's more. Jesus also came to the place where the prophet Ahijah lived and therefore where Jeroboam's wife received the prophecy her son would die. And, in recapitulating the old story of the torn-apart kingdom, that too must be undone. Jesus will have to retrace her steps from Shiloh to Tirzah and speak life to a dying son.

Shiloh is first mentioned in the messianic prophecy given by Jacob to his son Judah:

> *A sceptre will never depart from Judah nor a ruler's staff from between his feet until Shiloh comes and the people obey him.*
>
> Genesis 49:10^{GWT}

Because Shiloh is sometimes rendered as *peaceful* and also as *he whose it is*, an alternative translation is:

> *The sceptre will never depart from Judah, nor a ruler's staff from between his feet, until the One comes, who owns them both, and to him will belong the allegiance of nations.*
>
> Genesis 49:10^{ISV}

This is a curious prophecy. Does it imply the tribe of Judah will lose its rights to rulership when Shiloh, the Messiah, comes? When Jesus reunites the kingdom under Himself as the Son of David, is He going to bypass Judah entirely when He hands on David's mantle of kingship? Of course, Jesus has the right to bestow inheritance in any way He chooses, but our natural thinking is that He'd restore it to a descendant in the bloodline of David. Perhaps obscure, perhaps humble, but nonetheless of royal Judahite lineage.

Apparently, Jesus doesn't think like we do. After all, when it comes right down to it, the only king ever meant to rule in Israel was Yahweh Himself.

JOHN 4:1–6 ESV

Now when Jesus learned that the Pharisees had heard that Jesus was making and baptising more disciples than John (although Jesus Himself did not baptise, but only His disciples), He left Judea and departed again for Galilee. And He had to pass through Samaria. So He came to a town of Samaria called Sychar, near the field that Jacob had given to his son Joseph. Jacob's well was there; so Jesus, wearied as He was from His journey, was sitting beside the well. It was about the sixth hour.

JOHN 18:28 NIV

two

Then the Jewish leaders took Jesus from Caiaphas
to the palace of the Roman governor.
By now it was early morning,
and to avoid ceremonial uncleanness
they did not enter the palace,
because they wanted to be able to eat the Passover.

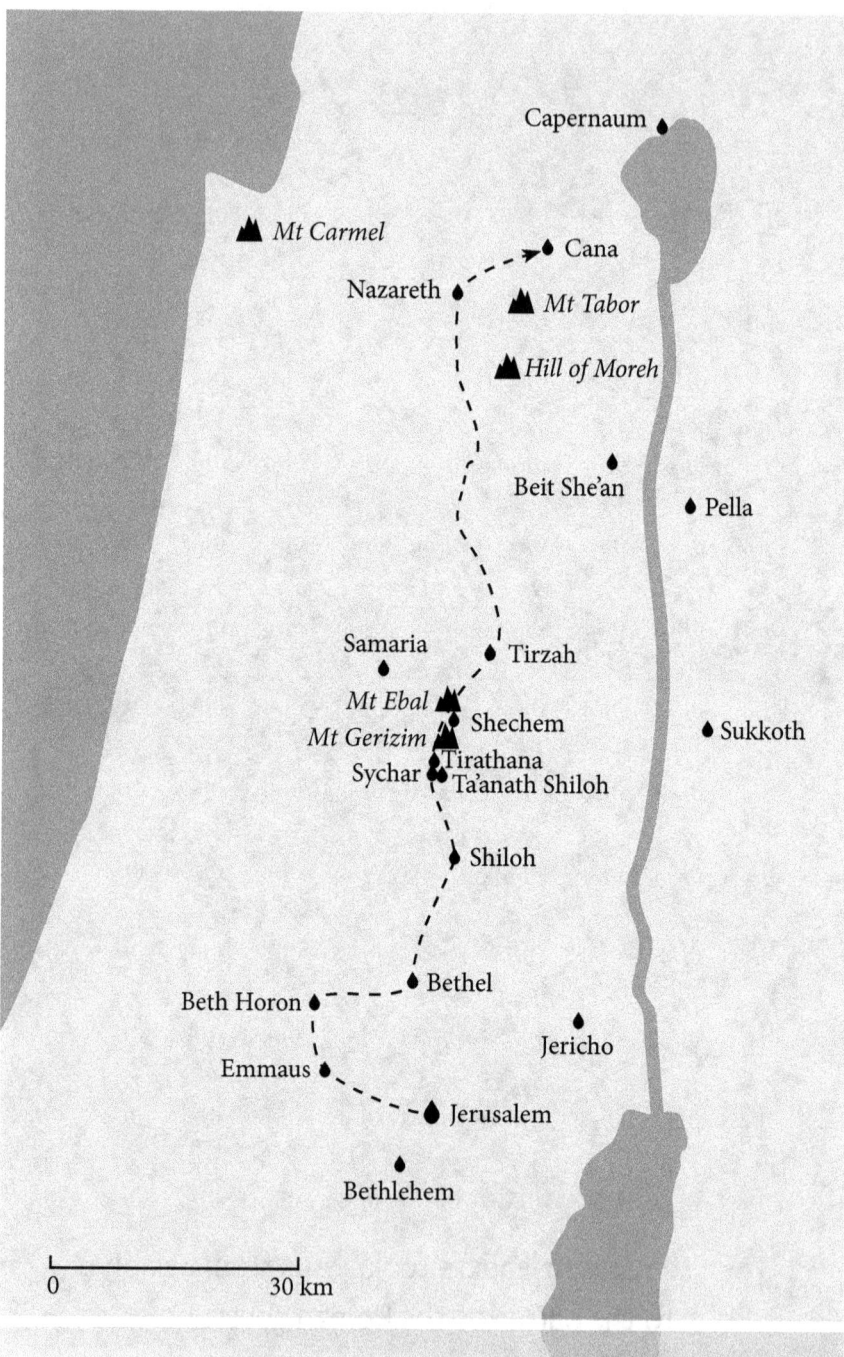

Route of Jesus

2.1 Cleanness

Now when Jesus learned that the Pharisees had heard that Jesus was making and baptising more disciples than John (although Jesus Himself did not baptise, but only His disciples), He left Judea and departed again for Galilee. And He had to pass through Samaria. So He came to a town of Samaria called Sychar, near the field that Jacob had given to his son Joseph.
John 4:1–5^{ESV}

Then the Jewish leaders took Jesus from Caiaphas to the palace of the Roman governor. By now it was early morning, and to avoid ceremonial uncleanness they did not enter the palace.
John 18:28^{NIV}

IN THESE CHIASTIC SECTIONS, there are five complementary aspects:

- a transitional movement from one location to another
  - from Judea to Samaria
  - from Caiaphas' house to the governor's palace
- entry to a space deemed as defiled because of foreign habitation
  - Samaria in the first case
  - the governor's palace in the second

- evocations of government
    - ▷ Shechem was the seat of the first government in the Promised Land. It was an inheritance given to Joseph, one-time governor of Egypt
    - ▷ Pilate is the Roman governor
- the time of the day is indicated
    - ▷ it is about the sixth hour when He sits by Jacob's Well
    - ▷ it is morning when the Jewish leaders took Jesus to Pilate
- concern about ceremonial cleanness
    - ▷ the Jews considered the Samaritans unclean
    - ▷ they considered entering Pilate's residence would make them unclean

John begins his record of the meeting between Jesus and the Samaritan woman by explaining why Jesus left Judea for Galilee. It seems that the Pharisees had decided that there was a competition between Jesus and His cousin John the Baptiser. They were obviously conducting a headcount for their own purposes. Jesus wasn't having any part in their games—nor in the defilement they were bringing to the people's sincere acts of repentance by creating a rivalry where there was none.

This introduction brings into focus the true nature of defilement and, as the chiasmus unfolds, both spiritual cleanness and uncleanness are compared and contrasted. Cleanness as Jesus indicates when He washes the disciples' feet is not about ritual purity, ceremonial washing or careful avoidance of impure objects. Instead it's about belief. The Jewish leaders were doing their utmost to stay procedurally clean so they could celebrate the Passover, but they would never achieve their goal while they remained in adamant unbelief.

On the other hand, the Samaritan woman was the epitome of uncleanness in the eyes of those very same Jewish leaders—she was a Samaritan, strike one; a woman, strike two; five-times married and living in a dubious sixth relationship, strike three. Yet, she is drawn into belief and, through the agency of the Living Water, is spiritually cleansed just as much as she would have been if she'd happened to join one of the queues to be baptised by either John or the disciples of Jesus.

2.2 Through Samaria

And He had to pass through Samaria.

John 4:4 ESV

John doesn't explain why Jesus *had* to pass through Samaria. It certainly wasn't the only route from Judea to Galilee. It wasn't even the most frequented path. It was, however, the shortest. If He was hurrying because He wanted to reach Galilee by a particular date, then at some point His plans underwent a significant change. Time ceased to matter, and He stayed two days with the Samaritans.

In a practical sense, there's no obvious reason for John's comment that Jesus *had* to go the way He did, as if He didn't have a choice in the matter. But in the spiritual sense, there are many reasons for this imperative. Jesus, the healer of history, had a divine appointment with a broken woman beloved by God who would become His first evangelist. She had no idea she was to play such a significant role. Nor could she have ever imagined that she'd been appointed as a kingmaker for her people. Shiloh had come, the Messiah was at the gates, but the announcement of His advent rested entirely on her choices.

The road to Sychar led through Bethel where Jacob had dreamt of the ladder between heaven and earth, then on to Shiloh (not Ta'anath Shiloh) where the men of Benjamin abducted girls from a dance to rebuild their tribe after the civil war, then through Shechem to Tirzah before coming out into the Jezreel Valley in southern Galilee. Shechem was the original capital of the northern kingdom under its first ruler, Jeroboam, before he moved to Tirzah.

Bethel links us back to the first chapter and Jesus' promise to Nathanael that he would see angels ascending and descending on the Son of Man. That statement evokes the dream of Jacob at Bethel about a ladder stretching between heaven and earth with angels coming and going on it. These words to Nathanael are chiastically linked with Jesus' statement to Mary the Magdalene in John 20:17 not to touch Him because He had not yet ascended to the Father.

Shechem is also linked to Jacob also since, after his return from Paddan-Aram and his meeting with Esau, he travelled through the land until he reached Shechem. There he camped, bought a plot of land for a hundred pieces of silver and dug a well. He and his wives buried their household gods there. Setting up an altar, he called it El Elohe Israel, *El is the God of Israel* or *mighty is the God of Israel*.[33] This was the very place where his grandfather Abraham had built his first altar in the land. Jacob finally chooses unilateral commitment. It's a back-to-the-beginning moment for him, not just in his personal relationship with God but his family's relationship as well.

After his daughter Dinah was raped by a local prince, Jacob moved from Shechem back to Bethel. The prince fell in love with Dinah and, in order to marry her, persuaded the citizens of Shechem to

---

33   Genesis 33:19–20

cut a covenant with Jacob and his sons. Simeon and Levi however violated the covenant their father had sworn by massacring all the male citizens.

Along with all the other repair jobs Jesus has on His plate at Shechem, so too is this deliberate covenant transgression as well as the violation of a woman.

2.3 The Sixth Hour

NORMALLY WHEN COMMENTATORS HIGHLIGHT the significance of the sixth hour in the encounter between Jesus and the Samaritan woman it's to mention she's an outcast, shunned by her community. It's noon, at least by Jewish reckoning. No one goes to a well in the heat of the day—they draw water in the cool of the early morning or when evening is about to fall. The woman's appearance at midday therefore signals that she's avoiding others, keeping her profile low, trying to fly under the radar, attempting to minimise the rejection she'll experience and the gossip she'll generate.

All very well, providing it's summer. But there's no mention of the season. I believe, based on the other significant reference to Living Water in John's gospel, that this meeting happens during Sukkot, the Feast of Tabernacles. That festival occurs during autumn, or fall, and while the temperature is not cold at that stage of the year, it's certainly not the scorching heat of summer either. Furthermore, there can be many practical reasons for the woman going to the well at noon that have nothing to do with her social status. She might be helping a neighbour, have run out of water unexpectedly, or simply have had a disrupted routine.

However, it's just as possible that the woman was indeed going to the well very early in the day. If John is using the Roman system of calculating time, starting at midnight, then the sixth hour during autumn in Israel is just after dawn. Now there is reason to believe that John was using the Roman measurement. The only way his account of the trial of Jesus and crucifixion can be harmonised with the descriptions in the synoptic gospels is by recognising he was referencing an alternative time system—one that a predominately non-Jewish audience would recognise.[34]

If the woman did indeed meet Jesus just after dawn, then the symbolism is intense. This foreshadowing of the encounter between Mary the Magdalene and Jesus after the resurrection signifies the coming of the Daystar, the sun, or is a figure of the Morning Star, the last star to fade into a brightening sky. Both the Daystar and the Morning Star are emblematic of Jesus:

> *We have also a more sure word of prophecy; whereunto you do well that you take heed, as to a light that shines in a dark place, until the day dawn, and the day star arise in your hearts.*
>
> 2 Peter 1:19[KJV2000]

> *I, Jesus, have sent My angel to give you this testimony for the churches. I am the Root and the Offspring of David, and the bright Morning Star.*
>
> Revelation 22:16[NIV]

Jesus, simply by His appearance at the well, stands in opposition to Resheph, the patron deity of Shechem in bygone days. The stag-god Resheph was considered the gatekeeper of the underworld and was apparently associated with the Morning Star, since in Hebrew the name of this bright planet was *'the deer at daybreak'*.

---

34   See: randomgroovybiblefacts.com/the_crucifixion_in_sync.html (accessed 19 April 2025)

This points to the title for the tune, *The Doe at Dawn,* of the Messianic psalm that so accurately prophesied the crucifixion: Psalm 22. This motif of the deer recalls the prophecy of Solomon in the very last line of Song of Songs:

> *Make haste, my beloved, and be like a gazelle or a young stag on the mountains of spices.*
>
> Song of Songs 8:14[ESV]

This prophecy, as noted in *The Lustral Waters,* the previous book in this series, looks to the staggering quantity of spices provided by Nicodemus and the women-disciples of Jesus at His tomb.

Now the stag-god Resheph was considered to be equivalent to Nergal, a war-god imported centuries previously into Samaria from a Mesopotamian town called Kutha. Nergal and Resheph were both associated with scorching heat: Nergal with searing sunlight and Resheph with flying sparks. Jesus has come to the heartland of the old-time worship of these ancient godlings of burning fire, bringing Living Water to douse their hold on power and provide refreshment for those thirsty for the Living God.

All this background and these possibilities notwithstanding, there's a much more profound reason for recalling it was the *sixth* hour than simply drawing attention to the woman's personal circumstances. Once we compare the scene where she appears with the trial before Pilate, we realise there's more in play. John only twice mentions the 'sixth hour', once here and once on the day Jesus was crucified:

> *Now it was the day of Preparation for the Passover. It was about the sixth hour. He said to the Jews, 'Behold your King!'*
>
> John 19:14[ESV]

It's not a perfect chiastic match, but it's close.

'Behold your King!' Pilate proclaimed to the people at this time.

Nothing could be plainer. The sixth hour heralds the king's unveiling.[35] John signals to us through this paired timing that both stories have the same theme: *kingship*.

---

35 The sixth hour, *noon*, on the day before the Passover is also significant as the time at which the Passover lambs began to be sacrificed in the Temple. According to Josephus, 256,500 lambs were slain at the Passover in 70 AD. The number is so great that not all could be butchered on the Passover itself. The discrepancy between John's gospel and the synoptics for the day of Jesus' death (the day before the Passover vs the Passover) can be explained by first century practice. There was an official Passover and a domestic Passover. The first century Jewish philosopher, Philo, recorded: 'The day called by the Hebrews in their own tongue, the Pasch [Passover], on the which the whole people sacrifice, every member of them, without waiting for the priests, because the law has granted to the whole nation for one special day in every year the right of priesthood and of performing the sacrifice themselves.' (Philo, *De Decalogue*) See: cbcg.org/booklets/the-christian-passover/chapter-seventeen-later-passover-practices-as-recorded-by-jewish-historians.html (accessed 12 February 2025)

2.4 Kingmakers

A KINGMAKER IS A PERSON WHO has the power to persuade others that their favoured candidate for the throne is the right choice. They themselves have no desire to aspire to the position or else they are aware they would never be accepted. They are generally influential prominent individuals.

Yet in the upside-down kingdom of heaven, influence and prominence appear to be an optional qualification for the role. Notoriety will apparently do as well. There are three kingmakers in John's gospel. Two of them appear in the chiasm that parallels the Samaritan woman with the Roman governor.

Pontius Pilate declared Jesus King. He did so more than once: he announced it on the pavement outside his palace and he wrote it out on an inscription that was nailed to the Cross. He is the kingmaker who represents the Gentiles.

But it was not sufficient for Jesus to be declared king merely by a representative of the Roman empire. In contemporary Jewish thinking, the world was divided into three parts: Jew, Gentile and Samaritan. Therefore Jesus had to be proclaimed king by legitimate representatives of all three groups in order to be acclaimed King of the World.

Now the woman Jesus met at Jacob's Well is, as we shall see, the kingmaker who represents the Samaritans. She persuades the people of her hometown to invite Jesus to stay in case He is the Messiah. In chapter thirteen, Mary of Bethany is shown to be the kingmaker for the Jews when she anoints Jesus on the evening before[36] He rides triumphantly into Jerusalem on a donkey.

It may seem inordinately strange that God would choose women as His kingmakers. In previous centuries, Samuel had been the kingmaker for both Saul and David, while Zadok and Nathan were kingmakers for Solomon. Elijah was assigned as the kingmaker for both Jehu of Israel and Hazael of Aram, but he did not complete this task.[37] Instead, according to Jewish tradition, Jonah was the young fast runner from the company of the prophets who was sent by Elisha to anoint Jehu.

Now these kingmakers are all men and they're almost all prophets.[38]

---

36   In Jewish reckoning the day starts at sundown. Mary's action during the evening therefore occurs *on the same day* as Jesus is acclaimed the 'Son of David', a royal title.

37   The widespread assumption that Elijah actually did fulfil the Lord's instructions to anoint Jehu, Hazael and Elisha is not borne out by the Scriptural record. There is complete silence on the matter. The view of those who notice this is best exemplified by various scholars who write that the Bible doesn't say Elijah performed the triple anointing but it doesn't say he didn't either and, furthermore, we cannot conclude from this absence of detail he did not complete his assigned task, so we should conclude he did. This is a logical fallacy that, if applied to other silences in Scripture, is often going to lead us astray. I believe, as outlined in *The Elijah Tapestry*, the first book in this series, that John in his gospel clearly indicates Jesus gave Peter the mantle and the unfinished assignment of Elijah to complete. It follows, therefore, that the triple anointing was not fulfilled during Elijah's own lifetime.

38   Perhaps they were all prophets, since the only one we don't know for sure about is Zadok who was classified as a priest but he may have been described that way simply to distinguish his role at the time from that of Nathan.

Yet, suddenly and mysteriously, Jesus overturns this long-established custom. Two of His three kingmakers are women, two of the three are also foreigners and not one of them is explicitly said to be a prophet.

The Samaritan woman may, however, actually qualify in that regard. John Loren Sandford points out that she was indeed likely to have been considered a prophet by her own people since divorce was exceedingly uncommon and her multiple husbands suggest she had been a widow five times. The tragic strangeness of those circumstances would indicate to her community the strong possibility she was a prophet.[39]

When it came to the role of women, it was perhaps natural for them to be chosen as kingmakers—at least when it came to divine kings, if not earthly ones. After all, Anat—the savage Canaanite war goddess Jesus had declared war on at Cana[40]—claimed the right to determine who amongst the gods was entitled to the throne of heaven and earth. Perhaps therefore Jesus looked for a woman able to step into the role of kingmaker, at the appointed hour, and thereby join Him in battle to oppose and overcome Anat—just as Deborah had done.

---

[39] John Loren Sandford and Paula Sandford, *The Elijah Task: A Call to Today's Prophets and Intercessors*, Spring Arbor Distributors 1980

[40] See: *The Summoning of Time*, the second book in this series.

2.5 The Samaritans and Nabataeans

The Samaritans in the time of Jesus were considered racially impure. When the Assyrians had invaded in 732 BC, they had taken the elite of the northern kingdom and deported them to various cities throughout their empire. These Israelites became known as the 'ten lost tribes'. To replace them, the Assyrians sent in outsiders, drawing them from five major centres—in particular from a city named Kutha.[41]

As a consequence, the Hebrew people used the term 'Kuthites' for the Samaritans.[42] The word 'Samaritan' is Greek, and derives from the Hebrew word for the name of a hill chosen by one of the northern kings for his new capital. The hill was Shomron, *watchtower*, after the original landowner Shomer, *watchman, guard*, or *keeper*.

However the Jews described these settlers who intermarried with those who had been left behind in the land as 'Kuthite', a term with derogatory overtones. The Samaritans were looked down on, partly because of their racial mixture and partly because when they first arrived, they naturally still worshipped the old idols from their homeland.

---

41   Also spelled Cuth, Cuthah, Cutha.
42   Alternatively 'Kuthim' or 'Cuthim', 'Cuthites' or 'Cuthaeans'.

> *But these various groups of foreigners also continued to worship their own gods. In town after town where they lived, they placed their idols at the pagan shrines that the people of Samaria had built. Those from Babylon worshipped idols of their god Succoth-benoth. Those from Cuthah worshipped their god Nergal. And those from Hamath worshipped Ashima. The Avvites worshipped their gods Nibhaz and Tartak. And the people from Sepharvaim even burned their own children as sacrifices to their gods Adrammelech and Anammelech.*
>
> *These new residents worshipped the Lord, but they also appointed from among themselves all sorts of people as priests to offer sacrifices at their places of worship. And though they worshipped the Lord, they continued to follow their own gods according to the religious customs of the nations from which they came.*
>
> 2 Kings 17:29–33^{NLT}

Now this might have been the Jewish view but it was certainly not the Samaritan view. By the time of Jesus, the Samaritans considered they had entirely cut themselves off from their former gods and had fully embraced the God of Israel—the land in which they lived. They therefore really were *Samaritans* in the oldest sense of the word: *keepers*. They saw themselves as *Keepers of the Law*. As a result, they only recognised the Torah as Scripture. They excluded from their canon the historical books, the psalms and songs, the prophets and writings. They considered the move of the worship centre from Shechem as ordained by Moses, to the Temple in Jerusalem as devised by David, to be an abandonment of the true faith. The Jews saw the Samaritans as engaged in a syncretic formulation of religion—mixing the worship of the Lord with that of other gods, but the Samaritans saw exactly the opposite. It was the Jews who were syncretic, and who accused others of the very abominable practices they themselves indulged in.

Now their pre-eminent deity back in Mesopotamia had been Nergal. His main cult centre was in Kutha. He was associated with war and disease; his emblems were bulls and lions.[43] However, according to rabbinic tradition, he was associated with the image of a foot or a rooster. His name was often joined together with that of the Canaanite stag-god, Resheph. So, given that it is known Resheph was considered to be the patron of Shechem, it is evident Nergal was too. Not simply because their names were frequently combined but because Nergal had been introduced with the coming of the Kuthites.

Kutha lies on the Upper Euphrates river, north-east of Babylon. Until the early twentieth century, it had been for millennia identified with a much more famous city: Ur of the Chaldees, Abraham's birthplace. In the twelfth century, the revered Jewish scholar and philosopher Maimonides wrote of Abraham being reared in Kutha.[44]

So, regardless of Ur's actual location, first-century Jews considered the Samaritans they so despised to be the disenfranchised kin of their forefather Abraham. The contempt was mutual. The Samaritans had taken on the Torah as well as worship of Yahweh

---

43   Nergal may possibly be the same as Melqart, *king of the city of the underworld.* See: en.m.wikipedia.org/wiki/Melqart (accessed 5 November 2024) If that is the case, then in this pericope about the Samaritan woman, the apostle John picks up a thread from the second chapter about the expulsion of the money-changers in the Temple. The image on the coin used for the Temple tax was Herakles-Melqart. See: *The Summoning of Time*, the second book in this series.

44   pathoftorah.com/2013/10/27/abrahams-journeys-ur-and-haran-part-1/ (accessed 5 November 2024) There was, admittedly, another main contender when it came to Ur—that was Edessa in Mesopotamian Aram, just fifty kilometres from Harran. If Edessa is correct, then Abraham's father didn't move very far at all before stopping and settling down in Harran.

but they refused to recognise the Temple in Jerusalem as the Lord's legitimate centre of worship.[45]

Now another group of people, who are also relevant to the fourth chapter of John's gospel, also claimed to have originated in Kutha. It's worthwhile keeping this much-overlooked group in mind. They were the Nabataeans, the inhabitants of Petra, now a famous tourist attraction in Jordan. In the first century, Petra was the capital of Arabia. When Saul, after encountering Jesus on the way to Damascus, says that he went first of all to Arabia, this is the place he meant. The Nabataeans were traders who made their fortune through commercial ties that extended from the far corners of the Roman Empire across the Indian Ocean to China.

During the lifetime of Jesus, the Nabataean king was Aretas IV. His daughter Phasa'el was Herod Antipas' first wife before she was divorced so Herod could marry Herodias, his step-brother's wife. John the Baptiser denounced Herod's action and was eventually beheaded for speaking out.

Jesus evidently went to Sychar before John was arrested, since we're told that Jesus left for Galilee when the Pharisees began comparing baptismal counts between Himself and John. And it is in Sychar He began to take sides against the prejudice of His own compatriots and countrymen with regard to the kind of worshippers the Father is seeking. He not only includes the marginalised Samaritans in the kingdom of heaven, but not long afterwards, He brings in the Nabataeans as well.

---

[45] See: philipharland.com/Blog/2022/10/samaritans-josephos-josephus-on-cuthean-origins-and-relations-with-judeans-over-centuries-late-first-century-ce/ (accessed 5 November 2024)

Chinese chronicles record that Petra, the Nabataean capital, changed its name at one point from Reqem[46] (which the Chinese pronounced 'Li-kan') to Butlem. This name was said to have been adopted from the birthplace of the King of kings and to have applied to the whole surrounding country. Friedrich Hirth in *China and the Roman Orient* suggests that Butlem is suspiciously like Bethlehem,[47] suggesting that the Nabataean authorities came to give their devotion to Jesus.

---

46 Petra is the modern name. Its ancient name in the local language was Reqem or Raqmu. It was also called Pel, Seir or Sela. The area was originally occupied by the Edomites, the descendants of Esau.

47 Friedrich Hirth, *China and the Roman Orient,* Ares Publishers, Chicago, 1975.

Part

John 4: 7–12 ESV

A woman from Samaria came to draw water.
Jesus said to her, 'Give Me a drink.'
(For His disciples had gone away into the city to buy food.)

The Samaritan woman said to Him, 'How is it that You, a Jew,
ask for a drink from me, a woman of Samaria?'
(For Jews have no dealings with Samaritans.)

Jesus answered her, 'If you knew the gift of God, and who it is
that is saying to you, "Give Me a drink," you would have asked Him,
and He would have given you living water.'

The woman said to him, 'Sir, you have nothing to draw water with,
and the well is deep. Where do you get that living water?
Are you greater than our father Jacob? He gave us the well and
drank from it himself, as did his sons and his livestock.'

So Pilate came out to them and asked,
'What charges are you bringing against this man?'

'If He were not a criminal,' they replied,
'we would not have handed Him over to you.'

Pilate said, 'Take Him yourselves and judge Him by your own law.'

'But we have no right to execute anyone,' they objected. This took place
to fulfill what Jesus had said about the kind of death He was going to die.

Pilate then went back inside the palace, summoned Jesus and asked Him,
'Are You the King of the Jews?'

'Is that your own idea,' Jesus asked, 'or did others talk to you about Me?'

'Am I a Jew?' Pilate replied. 'Your own people and chief priests
handed You over to me. What is it You have done?'

Jesus said, 'My kingdom is not of this world. If it were,
My servants would fight to prevent My arrest by the Jewish leaders.
But now My kingdom is from another place.'

'You are a king, then!' said Pilate.

Jesus answered, 'You say that I am a king. In fact, the reason I was born
and came into the world is to testify to the truth.
Everyone on the side of truth listens to Me.'

John 18:29-37 NIV

Three

3.1 Give Me Sychar

> *A woman from Samaria came to draw water. Jesus said to her, 'Give Me a drink.'*
>
> John 4:7[ESV]

Sychar and Shechem are very similar in Greek, Sychar being Συχαρ, and Shechem Συχεμ. However, they derive from different Hebrew words. Shechem, *shoulder*, denotes *government*. Sychar, *to drink*, has overtones of *wages* or *hire*.

When Jesus says, '*Give Me a drink,*' He's using a wordplay on the name of the nearest town. 'Give Me Sychar' is what He's proposing, declaring from His opening words to the woman that He's not so much looking for water as her city's allegiance.

The well is a sacred one. It was dug by Jacob and used by his sons, as the woman will inform Jesus—thereby telling Him that at least one of His ancestors, no matter which tribe He comes from, used and valued this place. Her words caution Him, despite His bold manner, to be respectful. Yet they also explain why there's no way for travellers to access the well. Because of its history and the hallowed overtones clinging to it, the local people have obviously decided to keep its waters from random defilement as best they can.[48] There is no bucket for strangers to use.

Visitors have to be humble and ask. Yet Jesus does not ask; instead He commands. Just as a king would.

---

[48] The fact the well is a sacred one is another reason that John Sandford in *The Elijah Task* suggests the woman was considered a prophet. If she were a notorious sinner, she would have been disbarred from the well since its waters were holy.

3.2 Deflection

(For His disciples had gone away into the city to buy food.) The Samaritan woman said to Him, 'How is it that You, a Jew, ask for a drink from me, a woman of Samaria?' (For Jews have no dealings with Samaritans.)
John 4:8–9^{ESV}

So Pilate came out to them and asked, 'What charges are you bringing against this man?' 'If He were not a criminal,' they replied, 'we would not have handed Him over to you.'
John 18:29–30^{NIV}

JESUS IS ALONE, WITHOUT HIS DISCIPLES, in both these incidents. He has no one looking on in disapproval at Jacob's Well and He has no one to defend Him in the praetorium of Pilate. Although Peter had followed Him into the courtyard of Caiaphas' palace, he had by this stage already denied Him three times.

Now the Samaritan woman apparently wanted to avoid Jesus' direct request for water. So too the Jewish leaders wanted to avoid Pilate's direct request to them to specify the charges being laid against Jesus. Neither the woman nor the leaders ignore the issue but both of them attempt a deflection in order to dodge it.

The Samaritan woman doesn't answer 'yes' or 'no'; she doesn't wordlessly hand Jesus a drink or walk silently away in order to come back later. Instead she begins to engage in open-ended conversation. She asks a question that can't simply be answered with a simple 'yes' or 'no'. Maybe she hoped a Jew would be put off by the prospect of a conversation with a woman—a Samaritan one at that. After all, the final breach between the Jews and the women of Samaria occurred during the governorship of Nehemiah over four centuries previously.

Nehemiah, the cupbearer to King Artaxerxes of Persia, had returned to Jerusalem to rebuild the city. Along with Ezra the priest, he'd enforced a strict policy of racial purity amongst the exiles who were living in Judah. Many of the Jewish men had married foreign wives, and some of the children of these unions didn't know how to speak Hebrew or Aramaic.[49] Nehemiah called down curses on the men and physically abused them. At the same time, Ezra led the people in a covenant to separate themselves from the nations around about them—an oath that included divorcing any foreign wives and sending them away, along with any children of the marriage.[50]

Although the woman of Samaria doesn't mention Nehemiah or Ezra, they are in the background of her entire conversation with Jesus. She may well have been thinking: you Jewish men banished us foreign women and swore you'd have nothing to do with us ever again. Don't you know the history between us, Mr Jew?

The Good News Translation of the parenthesis within verse 9 draws attention to cups and thus obliquely to cupbearers:

> *(Jews will not use the same cups and bowls that Samaritans use.)*

---

49   Although Nehemiah 12:23 only mentions the women of Ashdod, Ammon and Moab, it is clear the Samaritans are also included since in verse 28, Nehemiah records that he drove out the son-in-law of Sanballat, the Samaritan leader who lived in Beth Horon.
50   Ezra 10:1–44

It wasn't just that these different cultures didn't associate, the Jews considered Samaritans unclean. The Samaritans had rebuilt their temple on Mount Gerizim in the second century before Christ but the Jewish ruler John Hyrcanus, a king of the Maccabean line, had destroyed it in 110 or 111 BC. The Samaritans waited a century until Herod had rebuilt the Jerusalem Temple and then desecrated it at some time during the childhood of Jesus. They scattered human bones around the sacred precinct at the Passover. This outrage had occurred within the previous twenty years, so it would be well-remembered by the Jews. Possibly the family of Jesus had even present when it happened.[51] In addition to these tensions regarding the rival Temples, some rabbinic teachers were so prejudiced against the Samaritans that they classed their women as permanently unclean.[52]

So Jesus' words contain multiple levels of surprise:

- He's asking for a cup or drinking vessel that, coming from a Samaritan, Jews would normally smash rather than touch
- He's talking to a woman—strange enough if He's dressed to be recognised as a rabbi—but a *Samaritan* woman, that would make Him doubly unclean

She may have been avoiding Jesus' request but she didn't reject Him as a person. In that, she is a complete contrast to the Jewish leaders of His own people. They have totally rejected Him and

---

51   James F McGrath, *What Jesus Learned from Women*, Cascade Books, Oregon, 2021

52   A rabbinic law from the middle of the first century declared that Samaritan women were always menstruating, therefore ritually impure at all times. To be handed something by them would therefore defile the person who touched what they had touched. See: bible.org/seriespage/1-outcast-women-identified-lifestyle-samaritan-woman (accessed 20 January 2025)

branded Him a criminal. When Pilate tries to ascertain His crime, he's met with deflection and vagueness.

These two sections—the woman's reply to Jesus' question and the leaders' reply to Pilate's question—counterpoint each other. A foreigner is taking her first tentative steps into the embrace of the Spirit of God, while Jesus' fellow citizens are making their final move towards utter rejection of the Spirit.

3.3 Primal Echoes

Pilate said, 'Take Him yourselves and judge Him by your own law.'

'But we have no right to execute anyone,' they objected.

This took place to fulfill what Jesus had said about the kind of death He was going to die.

John 18:31-32^{NIV}

JOHN IS THE ONLY GOSPEL WRITER to feature this particular section of the dialogue between Pilate and the chief priests. He's drawing on the ancient echoes of a previous Passover sacrifice with the quote and the clue he provides us.

Back in John's second chapter, a quote from the Book of Genesis pointed us to the saga of Joseph. Reinforcing that quote was another, chiastically placed in the twentieth chapter, also from Joseph's story. Those two quotes were clues to:

- the recapitulation—the healing of history—that Jesus was undertaking
- the mantle Jesus was in the process of passing on

Joseph had seriously messed up when he dispossessed the Egyptians of their ancestral land and severed their ties to their heritage through forced resettlement. A millennium later his descendants reaped what he'd sown and were dispossessed of their tribal land and also had their ties broken through forced resettlement.

So now, we are presented with another quote that directs our attention to another ancient iniquity.

We are not permitted to execute anyone.	*It's not for us to execute anyone in Israel.*
John 18:31[NKJV]	2 Samuel 21:4[ISV]

The words are almost identical. The first set of words were directed to Pilate, the second set to King David. They are being carefully paralleled. David, it transpires, was—depending on the circumstances—just as wishy-washy and weak-willed as Pilate was.

Both stories involve innocent victims slain at the time of the Passover. Just as Joseph's descendants reaped what he had sown a millennium down the track so, in a similar time frame, Jesus as a descendant of David reaped what David had sown.

A famine occurred during David's reign and when he inquired of the Lord, he was told the cause was Saul's breach of covenant with the Gibeonites. Instead of protecting them as required under the terms of the ancient treaty with Joshua, Saul had massacred them. Desperate to end the famine, David asked the Gibeonites what they wanted in return for blessing the land.

> 'We're not looking for mere silver or gold to be paid by Saul or his household to us,' the Gibeonites responded to him. 'And it's not for us to execute anyone in Israel.'
>
> In reply, David asked, 'So what are you asking me to do for you?'
>
> 2 Samuel 21:4[ISV]

Just as the Gibeonites were legally restricted from sentencing anyone to death, so too were the first-century Jews by the Romans. The Gibeonites sought permission for human sacrifice from David who was, for them, a foreign overlord. In granting approval, he allowed them to kill their victims at the beginning of the barley harvest—that is, Passover. This eerily foreshadows the actions of Annas, Caiaphas and their supporters who sought permission from Pilate, a foreign overlord, for human sacrifice at the Passover. He too consented to the killing of an innocent victim.

With this clue, John reveals that these chiastic sections are about David, the trauma he brought upon the land through his decision, and what the inheritors of his mantle have to work through by way of repair. Both these sections are about kingship and power, what it really means and how it should be exercised.

In fact, the very next words in both dialogues—that with the woman and that with Pilate—move straight to the topic of kingship. With Pilate, the subject is so overt, it's unmissable; but with the woman, Jesus introduces the idea with extreme subtlety.

3.4 Living Water

Jesus answered her, 'If you knew the gift of God, and who it is that is saying to you, "Give Me a drink," you would have asked Him, and He would have given you living water.'

John 4:10^{ESV}

Pilate then went back inside the palace, summoned Jesus and asked him, 'Are You the king of the Jews?'

'Is that your own idea,' Jesus asked, 'or did others talk to you about Me?'

'Am I a Jew?' Pilate replied. 'Your own people and chief priests handed You over to me. What is it You have done?'

John 18:33–35NIV

'Am I a Jew?' Pilate asked.

'How is it that You, a Jew, ask for a drink from me, a woman of Samaria?' the woman asked.

Both questions emphasise the non-Jewishness of the speaker, their outsider status, their foreign background.

'Is that your own idea?' Jesus asks when Pilate queries whether He is a king. *'If you knew… who it is saying to you… you would have asked Him,'* Jesus says to the woman.

Implicit in both wordings is the question, 'Do you know who I am?' With Pilate, Jesus was much more direct than He was with the woman. He made a point of asking Pilate if he wants to know because of hearsay or because he himself has a sense, perhaps a mere suspicion, there's something more about the Prisoner in front of him. Is Jesus testing Pilate to find out if the Holy Spirit is working in him? Certainly, with the woman, He alludes to the Holy Spirit—though she wouldn't have known it—when He mentioned Living Water.

His offer of that gift came to pass a few years later. John no doubt remembered the woman when he and Peter returned to Samaria, after Philip[53] had evangelised the whole region. Perhaps it was then he heard the full story of the conversation at the well and realised its significance.

> *The apostles in Jerusalem heard that the people of Samaria had received the word of God, so they sent Peter and John to them. When they arrived, they prayed for the believers that they might receive the Holy Spirit. For the Holy Spirit had not yet come down on any of them; they had only been baptised in the name of the Lord Jesus. Then Peter and John placed their hands on them, and they received the Holy Spirit.*
>
> Acts 8:14–17[GNT]

When Jesus initially spoke to the woman about Living Water, there was no possibility she could have understood it as a reference to the Spirit of God. Her thinking would have been limited to the ancient notion of 'living water' as flowing, not stagnant—sourced in a natural spring, rainwater or a running stream. It was the kind of water used for a mikvah, a purification bath. A

---

[53] Whether this is Philip the apostle or Philip the deacon is not clear in the Book of Acts. Most commentators consider him to be Philip the deacon.

mikvah was used by women after menstruation, people who had become defiled in some way, anyone entering the Temple and by converts to Judaism.[54] Jesus was essentially offering the woman the cleansing of baptism.

Right at the beginning of this pericope, John made the point of saying that Jesus had been supervising His disciples as they baptised many people—more people than the famous reformer, John the Baptiser—apparently to alert us that this theme of baptism is not entirely gone. Here is Jesus throwing out the possibility to a Samaritan woman. He may have moved on from Judea but He was not diverted from the task at hand.

Now, living water was also important in another way. It was an essential element in the rite of kingship. To offer someone living water has connotations of spiritual cleansing but, much more than that, also of a coronation.

---

54 Examples of mikvah have been found around the perimeter of the Temple Mount in Jerusalem that would have been used for this purpose. See: redeemerofisrael.org/2015/01/living-waters-and-woman-at-well.html (accessed 7 November 2024)

3.5 The Well and the Pit

> *The woman said to Him, 'Sir, You have nothing to draw water with, and the well is deep. Where do You get that living water? Are You greater than our father Jacob? He gave us the well and drank from it himself, as did his sons and his livestock.'*
>
> John 4:11-12^{ESV}

When Jacob's Well is first described in verse 6, the Greek word used is 'pégé', meaning *a fountain, a spring, a flow of water, a well*. That same word, 'pégé', is used again in verse 14. But here, in verses 11 and 12, a different Greek word is introduced—'phrear', *pit* or *cistern*.

John had directly linked Jacob's Well to the inheritance given to Joseph, so with the word 'pit', we should be reminded of the moment when Joseph was taken captive by his brothers, bound, thrown into a cistern and then sold into slavery in Egypt.

Joseph is a type of Jesus, a foreshadowing of the Saviour. Jesus, in the chiastic scene with Pilate, is bound—having spent the night in a cistern dungeon in the palace of Caiaphas. He's been sold for thirty pieces of silver, while Joseph was sold for twenty. Joseph was taken to Egypt, 'the underworld' in Israelite thinking. And there he became a ruler whose foresight saved his family, the Egyptian people and the surrounding nations. Yet he also made a grave error in taking the ancestral land of the Egyptians and giving them no way to ransom it or to redeem themselves from slavery.

And so, with this subtle evocation of the story of Joseph through the use of the word *pit*, we return to the need for recapitulation on Jesus' part. This is not now about a return of inheritance but about ruling and reigning. After all, it was Joseph's dreams about ruling and reigning that provoked the venomous reaction of his brothers.

> *Jesus said, 'My kingdom is not of this world. If it were, My servants would fight to prevent My arrest by the Jewish leaders. But now My kingdom is from another place.'*
>
> *'You are a king, then!' said Pilate.*
>
> *Jesus answered, 'You say that I am a king. In fact, the reason I was born and came into the world is to testify to the truth. Everyone on the side of truth listens to Me.'*
>
> John 18:36–37[NIV]

The primary purpose of the earthly aspect of My kingship, declares Jesus, is to testify to the truth. That's what I was born for.

Back in the dialogue between Jesus and the Samaritan woman, Jesus will soon declare that genuine worship of God as King of the Universe is done in Spirit and in truth.

John has thus threaded in a new element to the new birth he spoke about in the pericope involving Nicodemus—through water and the spirit. Now he weaves in truth, paralleling water, the Living Water of the Holy Spirit. It won't be until the seventh chapter that John will specifically equate the Living Water with the Holy Spirit. However he is seeding the ideas early on, tending them occasionally so they remain within our awareness until he is ready to unveil the connection between the Spirit, water, truth, new birth and kingship.

But this kingship is not autocratic—Jesus' rule bears no resemblance to David's monarchy or Joseph's term as viceroy. He came to serve, not to be served. He came to give His life in sacrifice, not to expect others to be the sacrifice for Him. He came to restore inheritances, not confiscate them. His kingship is one of rescue and release into freedom and truth. He pulls us from the pit and offers us water from the wellspring of Life.

3.6 The Wife at the Well

Throughout the folklore of many countries, particularly in lands settled by the Celts, there are tales of the hero who travels to a far country and, driven by thirst, finds himself bargaining for a drink with a woman protecting a sacred well. It's so common a motif that it's designated in the Aarne-Thompson-Uther Index of the folktale catalogue as type number 480.

The woman, so it eventually transpires in most stories, is able to bestow on the hero the kingship of the country. She's an archetype that goes back to a goddess of sovereignty. The hero, on the other hand, has a destiny to become the ruler of the land but he can't achieve his calling without her cooperation. Often she's a 'loathly lady', and thus in every way the opposite of the beautiful fairytale princess that we've been brought up to expect is going to be the hero's reward.

Now many such stories originate in the old, old myths of godlings and goddesses—and those legends both point to, and point away from, the Son of the Most High God. The Egyptian myth of Isis and Osiris, for example, at least as interpreted by Plutarch, the high priest of the Delphic Oracle near Corinth in Greece, presents time as the wife of water, and space as the wife of dryness.[55] In that curious description, we have echoes of Sychar and Jerusalem—since *appointed time* is a theme of John's gospel

---

55   Guy Davenport, *Geography of the Imagination: 40 Essays*, Basic Books, 1997

from Cana through to the well at Sychar and then back to Cana, while *dryness* is the meaning of 'Zion'.

These cross-cultural legends are highly-charged counterfeits of all that is spiritually real and authentic, and their resemblance to genuine truth can either awaken our hearts to the coming of Jesus or dull it so that He seems too ordinary to be the ultimate Hero—and that all other heroes are merely pale imitations of Him.

Now the Samaritan woman bears no resemblance whatsoever to any perfect princess model that might be lurking at the back of our minds because we've imbibed too many fluffy Disney makeovers of old, dark fairytales. Instead:

- ✓ She's a foreigner, and so she ticks the 'far country' box.
- ✓ She's definitely not an unmarried maiden, so she ticks the 'loathly lady' box.
- ✓ She's at a cistern that, in ancient times, was dug by the revered patriarch Jacob, and therefore ticks the 'guardian of the sacred well' box.
- ✓ She doesn't immediately fall in with Jesus' request for some water but argues the point, thereby ticking the 'bargaining for a drink' box.
- ✓ And she's also the one who facilitates a gift of kingship to Jesus. Like the protectors of those legendary wells of folklore and fairytale, she represents the land, its complex history, and all the sovereignty that goes with it.

There are many echoes in her encounter with Jesus that hark back to various faith heroes meeting their brides. In fact, John has deliberately set up this motif of bride and bridegroom by closing off his third chapter with several statements by John the Baptist about being a friend of the Bridegroom who has great joy in listening for His voice and about how Jesus must become greater and he must become less.

John has pointed us to the substantial Scriptural record of significant meetings at wells. The Samaritan woman is the fifth in this historic line. Five is such an important number in this story. She has not only had five husbands, the land has known five men who covenanted at this location. The Samaritan people were said to be descended from the inhabitants of five cities in the Assyrian empire.

Now back in the time of the patriarchs, Eleazar, the servant of Abraham, was seeking a bride for his master's son Isaac and found Rebekah by a well in Paddan-Aram—in today's southern Turkey. A far country, at least for him and his camels bearing gifts. A generation later Jacob, Isaac's son, was fleeing his twin brother's murderous anger when he came to a well—quite possibly the very same well where his grandfather's servant Eleazar first met his mother. There Jacob fell in love with the beautiful Rachel.[56] Moses, in a later age, also met his bride Zipporah by a well when he was fleeing the murderous rage of Pharaoh's officials.

The very first mention of a well and a wife in Scripture prefigures the meeting between Jesus and the Samaritan woman. It's the encounter between Hagar and the Angel of the Lord.

Hagar was Sarah's maidservant. She was a foreigner, a slave, and an abused woman. She was apparently nothing more than a commodity in the eyes of her mistress since Sarah never refers to Hagar by name but only as *'that slavewoman'* or *'my handmaiden'*.

Although God had promised Abraham and Sarah a son, Sarah was barren. She concluded the only way this promise could be

---

[56] Genesis 29:7 reveals that Jacob first met Rachel at a well around about midday, thus linking the sixth hour (though perhaps in different time systems) of the story of Jesus meeting the woman at a well dug by Jacob back to the patriarch of all twelve tribes. Within the gospel's broader theme of Jesus as the Bridegroom, John is pointing out that Jesus made sure the lost tribes of Israel were enfolded back into place as the bride of the King.

fulfilled was by giving her servant to her husband as his second wife. Technically, any child born to Hagar was Sarah's. Hagar was soon expecting and, as a consequence, she began to look down on Sarah. In reaction Sarah treated her even more harshly—the abuse intensifying to such a degree that Hagar fled into the wilderness to escape. There, by a spring of water in the desert, the Angel of the Lord found her. The angel's first word, significantly, is her name. The name that Sarah never used.

It's no wonder Hagar called God *'the Living One who sees me'*. She named the spring 'Beer Lahai Roi', *the well of the Living One who sees me*. The very first vision of God's nature was given to a desperate and broken woman. She doesn't make it into the long list of the heroes of the faith in Hebrews 11, yet she proclaimed a mystery endorsed by Abraham, Moses and Jesus.

In naming the well 'Beer Lahai Roi'—*the well of the Living One who sees me*—she also named God.[57] Her declaration calls to mind the name God disclosed to Moses at the burning bush, I AM WHO I AM or *I will be who I will be* or *the Existing One* or *the Ever-living One*. That last variation, *Ever-living One*, confirms to us that Hagar discerned an essential truth about God. It is also reminiscent of Yahweh Yireh, the name Abraham gave to God. Usually that is translated *the Lord who provides* but it can also be *the Lord who sees my need*.

Hagar didn't know the name 'Yahweh' but nevertheless she discerned in the Holy One sufficient truth of His divine nature to call Him 'Lahai Roi'. Her meeting with the angel on the road to Shur[58] is prophetic of the woman of Samaria meeting the Giver of

---

57 Genesis 16:13–14
58 It's possible the well called 'Beer Lahai Roi' is close to Petra, near the business quarter called 'Little Petra'. See: thetorah.com/article/locating-beer-lahai-roi (accessed 14 December 2024)

Living Water on the road to Sychar. Hagar is the first in a line of five biblical women who meet a man by a well who will change their destiny. The next was Rebekah, then Rachel, then Zipporah and, then, last but by no means least, the Samaritan woman.

Three of these five were abandoned through death or divorce. Hagar was divorced in order to disinherit her son Ishmael of the birthright of the firstborn. Legally, in that era, that was the only way it could be done. Zipporah was divorced after some forty years of marriage for unknown reasons.[59] Her sons were sent away with her. Both these women were foreigners, not part of the wider family of Israel. Like the women divorced by their husbands at the command of Nehemiah and Ezra, they were outsiders.

The Samaritan woman was also an outsider, a stranger, a foreigner, a wary and marginalised woman. She too came to a well and was astonished to be seen.[60] Her guarded heart opened as she gradually came to the realisation that she was seen by the Messiah Himself.

---

59 It's interesting to reflect on the possible ulterior motives of Moses in permitting divorce. Perhaps Jesus was obliquely commenting on the hardness of Moses' own heart in divorcing Zipporah and then marrying a woman from Cush when He remarked: *'Moses, because of the hardness of your hearts, permitted you to divorce your wives, but from the beginning it was not so.'* (Matthew 19:8[NKJV]) So, did Jesus, in His extensive recapitulation of the past events, address this wound too? It's impossible to be sure; however, there are strange hints in early Christian writings that Joseph, the foster-father of Jesus, had ancestry that included Zipporah's father. These writings will be examined in the next book in this series, *Bathing in Bronze*. Certainly, if that particular bloodline identification is correct, then Joseph's decision not to divorce Mary would be part of the healing recapitulation.

60 Although she doesn't fit the pattern of the foreign woman at the well, Hannah does fit partially into the framework of the rejected woman who comes to a sacred place. It was at Shiloh her prayer for a son was answered. It's therefore possible to suggest that the kingdom starts with her: she, after all, births the prophet who will anoint the first two kings of Israel after his sons are rejected as his successors by the people. God tells Samuel that the real rejection is of Himself as king.

3.7 The King's Cupbearer

The concern of Ezra and Nehemiah for racial purity amongst the returned exiles had a righteous motivation:

> *Was it not because of marriages like these that Solomon king of Israel sinned? Among the many nations there was no king like him. He was loved by his God, and God made him king over all Israel, but even he was led into sin by foreign women.*
>
> Nehemiah 13:26^{NIV}

However, their solution to the problem was not righteous. Nor was it, as we can see from Jesus' actions, what God wanted. When we judge Ezra and Nehemiah, or for that matter Abraham, Moses or any other faith hero, on their undoubted genuine personal integrity and exonerate them on that basis, we're apt to mistakenly think God approved of their actions—when sometimes that's far from the case. Jesus is the touchstone through which we can view God's judgment on the past. Unless we look to Him and how He deals with the events of history, we will not understand God's will for the situation.

There are 111 men listed in the Book of Ezra who agreed to divorce their foreign wives. That number tally alone should have given both Ezra and Nehemiah pause. It should have alerted them to another option—one other than divorce. Numbers like 111 and 1111 and 11111 are symbolic of *covenant*.[61]

That's the option that should have been presented to the women. *Covenant* with us like Ruth, the Moabite wife of Boaz, did. *Covenant* with us like Bithiah, the Egyptian wife of Mered and daughter of Pharaoh, did. *Covenant* with us like Rahab, the Canaanite prostitute and wife of Salmon, did. *Covenant* with us like Zipporah, the Midianite wife of Moses, did.[62] Choose *covenant*.

Ezra and Nehemiah were just plain wrong.[63] They did not give the foreign women the option of uniting with the people of Israel in the bonds of covenant. They simply sent them away with their children. Jesus begins His recapitulation of the story of Nehemiah with His opening words to the woman: *'Give Me a drink.'*

---

61   I'm aware you won't find this explanation of 111 and 1111 in the standard resource book about the spiritual meanings of numbers by EW Bullinger, *Number in Scripture*. However, it will be obvious this is its meaning when we look at the numerical underpinnings of John's seventeenth chapter in a forthcoming volume in this series.

62   And like the wives of the patriarchs, the twelve sons of Jacob, did. Although we don't know most of their names, the wives of *all* the patriarchs were non-Hebrews. Most were probably Canaanites (like Judah's wife and his daughter-in-law Tamar) though there might have been Ishmaelites, Midianites and Medanites in the mix. Joseph married Asenath, an Egyptian. There is no indication that Jacob sent back to Paddan-Aram for wives for his sons and surely, if he had, it would have been mentioned. In fact, just to make what Jesus is doing at Shechem even more interesting, it may well have been the women of Shechem taken by Levi and Simeon after they massacred the men of the town who became the wives of the patriarchs.

63   Although foreign women were the most significantly marginalised group after the exile, all women were increasingly excluded. David in Psalm 68:11[NIV] tells us: 'The Lord announces the word, and the women who proclaim it are a mighty throng.' However, 'after the exile, there was a fundamental shift to reduce women's participation. Herod's temple had a court for the women which did not exist in the Tabernacle or Solomon's temple. They could now be grouped with children and slaves.' Edgar Stubbersfield, *Women in Ministry: Paul's Advice to Timothy in its Historical Setting*, Wipf and Stock, 2022

In that moment, He offered her Nehemiah's mantle as well as the high office he once held—that of cupbearer to the 'king of kings'. In Nehemiah's case, he served Artaxerxes who was the fifth 'king of kings' of the Achaemenid Empire.[64] But in the woman's case, it is not just any king of kings, but THE King of kings who was extending this grant.

She is therefore not just a kingmaker but also a cupbearer. She hasn't brought up any question of covenant yet, and neither has Jesus. Still, it's coming. As both kingmaker and cupbearer, we should see in the woman far, far more than a counterpart to Nehemiah.[65] She's in a war zone and has stepped up and into the position that the goddess Anat had claimed as her own: both cupbearer to Baal-Hadad and kingmaker amongst the 'young lions' of the Canaanite pantheon.

---

64 The Book of Ezra records a letter from Artaxerxes that opens as follows: 'Artaxerxes, king of kings, To Ezra the priest, teacher of the Law of the God of heaven: Greetings.' (Ezra 7:12[NIV])

65 Amongst the more subtle echoes of the past that resonate in the background of the chiastic partnership is the story of Nehemiah's treatment of the returned exiles. (Nehemiah 13:25) Nehemiah went around beating the men who'd married foreign women and pulling out their hair. Isaiah 50:6 speaks of beating and the pulling out of a beard in his prophecy of the suffering of the Messiah. Although the beard-pulling is not mentioned in any gospel, it would have been a routine part of the beating mentioned by John in this section. The torture by the soldiers was, therefore, not merely a fulfilment of prophecy but part of the recapitulation of Nehemiah's governorship by Jesus.

3.8 Lord of the Covenant

> *'Are You greater than our father Jacob? He gave us the well and drank from it himself, as did his sons and his livestock.'*
>
> John 4:12[ESV]

THE MENTION OF JACOB, his sons and his livestock at Shechem are a reminder of the massacre of the locals by Simeon and Levi. The local prince, Shechem son of Hamor, saw Jacob's daughter Dinah, raped her and fell in love with her. By his own admission, he was willing to do anything to marry her and so persuaded the male citizens of the town to agree to the proposal put forward by Jacob's sons that they all be circumcised. He convinces them to do this by pointing out their livestock and property would become part of the town's holdings.

Although the story does not specifically use the word 'covenant', it's clear by both the requirement for circumcision and the understanding that the flocks and herds would be amalgamated with the town's, that this was a covenant arrangement. This explains why Jacob was so horrified by the massacre that he bypassed both Simeon and Levi for the blessing of the firstborn once Reuben had forfeited it. Jacob was rightly fearful that the people of the land would turn against him and his family once it became known they were covenant-breakers.

Covenant violation was one of the most shocking and shameful offences possible in the ancient world. Someone who breached covenant could never be trusted again—because, if that person could justify one betrayal, they could justify any other. In many cultures, the punishment for oath-breaking that involved covenantal pledges was death or exile. Even in the English-speaking world, this was true. The original word for someone who broke covenant was *warlock*—a term that came to mean *outlaw* because oath-breakers were so often cast out of society.

Despite this abuse of a covenantal agreement by Jacob and his sons, this became hallowed ground—the place of the well, the tree and the stone.

That's why Moses repeatedly told the people to go to Shechem,[66] and never even mentioned Jerusalem. Shechem was already established as a place for covenant reaffirmation by the patriarchs. Recall that it was here, under an oak,[67] that Abraham had built the first of seven altars when he entered the land God promised to his descendants. It was also here that Jacob, probably under that same oak, buried his household gods and rededicated himself to God with an altar to EL ELOHE ISRAEL. It was here that Joseph asked to be buried—on the plot of land his father especially bequeathed him, thereby reaffirming his allegiance to the Hebrew people and allaying his father's fears that he'd become completely Egyptian.

---

66 The instructions Moses gave to the people telling them to go to Shechem may have been issued at what is now Petra, the famous tourist attraction in Jordan. In the first century, it was the capital of Arabia and is therefore likely to be the place Paul went to for three years after he became a Christian. As previously mentioned, it may also be site of Beer Lahai Roi, the well where Hagar encountered the angel of God.

67 The Hebrew word is 'elah' and, although often translated *oak*, it may actually mean *terebinth*.

Joshua, in obeying the instructions of Moses, twice called on the people to ratify their covenant with God here, calling on a stone pillar as a witness. And it was here that Abimelech, son of Gideon, became the first king *in* Israel if not *of* Israel.

It had a nearby Temple to Baal-Berith, *the lord of the covenant*. Possibly Baal-Berith was equivalent to the Persian god of friendship and alliance, Mithra, *lord of the contract* or *lord of the covenant*. By the time of Jesus, Mithra had morphed into Mithras, the so-called *Invincible Sun*, a favourite patron of Roman legionnaires.

Possibly it is a relationship between Baal-Berith and Mithras, whose seven grades of initiation[68] included the crowned whip-bearing Sun-runner, that was the inspiration behind the name Photini that has been given by the Eastern Orthodox church to the Samaritan woman. The name means *light* or *enlightened*.

Orthodox writers point out that it is exceedingly unlikely this woman was divorced five times or that she was an adulteress. Women of the time did not have the right to divorce. It would have been a husband's decision. And no man would have been willing to marry her after that and bring shame on his family. And, even if such an exceptional man existed, it's beyond credibility to think there'd be a third and a fourth, let alone a fifth. But five times widowed? Such a series of calamities would have given her a reputation as either a cursed woman or a prophet who was probably married to a very elderly man originally, and after that by Levirate custom to his brothers one by one—all to keep her dowry in the family. But it speaks to a heart-breaking and tragic life.

Photini's five husbands are representative of the five men who reaffirmed covenant on this spot in ancient times. Perhaps too

---

68 These are possibly connected to the seven planets of the ancient world.

they are representative of the five cities from which the Samaritans trace their heritage. And perhaps she is representative of the five brides the Scriptural heroes met at a well.

What is the significance of this *five*?

Now Hebrew is an alphanumeric language, meaning that there are no separate numbers. Consequently it's the fifth letter, the 'hei', that requires consideration. 'Hei' represents the *breath of God*—pointing to the Holy Spirit, the Living Water, the seal of God's covenant. Once that seal was circumcision[69] but now it is the Spirit of God,[70] who is God's deposit and guarantee that the inheritance He promised will be ours.[71] Jesus is our covenant defender and also the One who cleanses the mantles passing from one generation to the next.

---

69   Romans 4:11
70   2 Corinthians 1:22
71   Ephesians 1:14

PART

Jesus said to her,
'Everyone who drinks of this water will be thirsty again,
but whoever drinks of the water that I will give him will never be thirsty again. The water that I will give him will become in him a spring of water welling up to eternal life.'

The woman said to Him,
'Sir, give me this water, so that I will not be thirsty or have to come here to draw water.'

Jesus said to her,
'Go, call your husband, and come here.'

The woman answered Him, 'I have no husband.'

Jesus said to her, 'You are right in saying, "I have no husband," for you have had five husbands, and the one you now have is not your husband. What you have said is true.'

The woman said to Him,
'Sir, I perceive that You are a prophet. Our fathers worshipped on this mountain, but You say that in Jerusalem is the place where people ought to worship.'

John 4:13-21 ESV

FOUR

'What is truth?' retorted Pilate. With this he went out again to the Jews gathered there and said, 'I find no basis for a charge against Him. But it is your custom for me to release to you one prisoner at the time of the Passover. Do you want me to release "the king of the Jews"?'

They shouted back, 'No, not Him! Give us Barabbas!' Now Barabbas had taken part in an uprising.

Then Pilate took Jesus and had Him flogged. The soldiers twisted together a crown of thorns and put it on His head. They clothed Him in a purple robe and went up to Him again and again, saying, 'Hail, king of the Jews!' And they slapped Him in the face.

Once more Pilate came out and said to the Jews gathered there, 'Look, I am bringing Him out to you to let you know that I find no basis for a charge against Him.' When Jesus came out wearing the crown of thorns and the purple robe, Pilate said to them, 'Here is the man!'

As soon as the chief priests and their officials saw Him, they shouted, 'Crucify! Crucify!'

But Pilate answered, 'You take Him and crucify Him. As for me, I find no basis for a charge against Him.'

The Jewish leaders insisted, 'We have a law, and according to that law He must die, because He claimed to be the Son of God.'

John 18:38–19:7 NIV

4.1 David Dancing

'No one is good except God alone.'

Mark 10:18^{ESV}

I'VE ONLY QUOTED THIS COMMENT by Jesus once so far in this book, so it's time for a reminder. Nowhere are we more in need of this than when it comes to the golden boy of Scripture—David of Bethlehem. He's the hero *par excellence*, the runt of the litter who becomes a champion, the underdog who triumphs over a hostile giant and a jealous king, he's the ordinary shepherd boy who braves a fearsome foe and, keeping his integrity in the face of massive temptation, eventually rises to such heights he's crowned king of all Israel. He lives in God's favour—and, but for one major moral lapse when he spots a beautiful woman and falls in lust with her, he's an exemplary man of faith. His songs have lasted right through the ages—his words of praise and wonder, confession and repentance have endured across three millennia. His Shepherd psalm is beloved by millions.

He's such an influential figure that the prophecies about the Messiah naturally look forward to the reinstatement of a kingship like his. The Jews of the first century were looking for a ruler in the mould of David. The messianic title, 'Son of David', led them to believe that the glory of David's throne would return in earthly power.

For many believers today, the only dark stain on David's monarchy is his adulterous liaison with Bathsheba. We're well overdue for a wake-up call on that particular idea. We've bought into David's own assessment of himself at the end of his life:

> *If my house were not right with God, surely He would not have made with me an everlasting covenant, arranged and secured in every part; surely He would not bring to fruition my salvation and grant me my every desire.*
>
> 2 Samuel 23:5^{NIV}

David is not just back-formulating a justification for the dubious deeds of his life and suggesting, 'I *must* have been righteous, because God favoured me,' he's declaring that his house, his descendants, are obviously going to be equally righteous because God promised an everlasting covenant. This is a complete failure to understand the nature of grace.[72]

Moreover, the House of David as a kingship covering all the tribes only lasted another generation. His grandson Rehoboam was essentially reduced to tribal headship. True, Rehoboam had a magnificent Temple and a glorious capital to enhance his rule but nothing was left of the united brotherhood that had once characterised the Israelites. In the natural, the everlasting covenant that secures the House of David is meaningless. Only in the spiritual does it make any sense.

On the surface, it would appear that the critical moment when the united monarchy fell apart was when Rehoboam unwisely promised to increase the burden his father Solomon had placed on the Israelites. Now Solomon is described in Scripture in exactly the same terms as the taskmaster Pharaoh of Egypt in

---

72   It's perhaps important to distinguish between 'righteous' and 'good'. One does not equal the other.

the days of the ten plagues.[73] He was a slave-driver who built the Temple through forced conscription, not freewill labour. All the gifts that had been given for the building and decoration of the Tabernacle back during the time of the wilderness wanderings had been voluntary, but coercion and deprivation were the order of the day when it came to the Temple. Even the king of Tyre felt underwhelmed when Solomon granted him some land and villages by way of recompense.

And, with respect to those land and villages, was it a righteous action on Solomon's part for some of the territory God had promised His people to be bartered off for fittings and furnishings of a Temple God didn't want? Solomon was wise in his early years, cruel in his middle years and unfaithful to God in his later years. Rehoboam started out ill-advised and harsh—telling the people that his father had scourged them with whips but he would do so with scorpions.

With that statement, ten of the twelve tribes rebelled. David's kingdom was torn asunder, never to be re-unified until Jesus,

---

73   Solomon married Pharaoh's daughter (1 Kings 3:1), who remains unnamed in the chronicle, as does the sister-in-law of Pharaoh who married Solomon's rival Jeroboam. Naamah was the wife of Solomon who was the mother of his heir, Rehoboam. She was from Ammon, the territory that had been conquered by Joab on behalf of David. (1 Kings 14:21) Perhaps Pharaoh's alliance with Jeroboam was influenced by some denied expectation on his part that, regardless of firstborn status, his grandchild would sit on the throne of the House of David. After all, Solomon had been a seventh son, not the firstborn. When it became clear that Solomon's heir would not be half-Egyptian, Pharaoh's attitude may well have changed. Solomon built many shrines for his wives, including one to Moloch, the fire-god of the Ammonites who demanded child sacrifice. (1 Kings 11:7) Presumably this particular shrine was for Naamah.

While we're on the subject of Egyptians and wives, it should be noted that many of the Pharaohs married their sisters. A comparison can be drawn with Abraham who also married his sister.

as a descendant of the line of David, came to Sychar to restore the kingdom.

Now, as I said, on the surface it would appear that the critical moment when the united monarchy is lost happens when Rehoboam's pride and elitism gets the better of him. But perhaps Rehoboam's arrogance wasn't the decisive factor. Perhaps it was David's.

> *Jesus said to her, 'Everyone who drinks of this water will be thirsty again, but whoever drinks of the water that I will give him will never be thirsty again. The water that I will give him will become in him a spring of water welling up to eternal life.'*
>
> John 4:13–14^{ESV}

The Greek word for *welling up* or *springing up*, 'hallomai', is a highly unusual choice here. Normally it refers to people, never to things like water.[74] It therefore denotes that the water is *living*—not in the ancient and traditional Jewish understanding that simply meant *flowing* and *not static*, but rather in the sense of an animate and personal being. John is already hinting at the revelation he will later unveil: the living water is the Holy Spirit.

However, 'hallomai' is also a technical term in Greek for a *jump* or a *leaping movement* in a dance.[75] So, in the context of a recapitulation of David's story, it can only refer to the time he leapt and danced before the Ark of the Covenant while bringing it into Jerusalem. Jesus is intent on healing the debacle that resulted from David's desire to bring the Ark to the city named for himself.

---

74 Brian Simmons, *The Book of John: Eternal Love*, Broadstreet Publishing 2019
75 See: encyclopediaofancientgreekdance.raftis.org/search/ (accessed 28 September 2024)

Because we read with the hero and not with the text, we tend to think David is commended for his exuberant worship because we are led to believe Michal is punished by God with barrenness for her contemptuous criticism. However, she's not punished by God but by David. Unlike several women in the Bible described as barren, this is not a word used for Michal. We're told she had no children. In other words David abandoned her. He had at least seven other wives and ten concubines, so it wasn't as if it was going to be a hardship for him.

Moses, in writing the Torah, recognised that the people would eventually crave a king. So certain rules were laid down half a millennia before David came to the throne.

> *He must not take many wives, or his heart will be led astray. He must not accumulate large amounts of silver and gold. When he takes the throne of his kingdom, he is to write for himself on a scroll a copy of this law, taken from that of the Levitical priests. It is to be with him, and he is to read it all the days of his life so that he may learn to revere the Lord his God and follow carefully all the words of this law and these decrees and not consider himself better than his fellow Israelites and turn from the law to the right or to the left.*
>
> Deuteronomy 17:17–20^{NIV}

Now, if David did as commanded and wrote out the Torah by hand and meditated on it every day, there's quite a bit he overlooked. His psalms proclaim his love of the Law[76] but there are significant gaps he didn't observe. There's the direct command here not to take too many wives. In a curious attempt to absolve David of transgressing this divine command, various rabbis across the ages have maintained that eight wives and ten

---

76 The psalms attributed to David that mention the 'law' are Psalms 19, 37 and 40. Psalm 119, though traditionally said to be written by David, is anonymous.

concubines[77] is not *'many'*! Not *many* compared with Solomon, perhaps, but that's about all. How we wriggle and squirm trying to squeeze our 'faith heroes' into the righteous superhuman mould we've assigned to them.

In addition to this command, there's also the directions for how to carry the Ark of the Covenant—David's failure to observe this led to the death of Uzzah. There's also the direction that a priest must not approach the altar on steps, but by a ramp, just to prevent him accidentally exposing himself. The principle behind that direction is that scrupulous decency is to be observed around the Ark of the Covenant.

And that principle might as well not have existed while David was dancing. He was lewd and exhibitionist.

David brought the Ark to Jerusalem with sacrifices every few steps and with wild, ecstatic dancing. Apparently his cavorting would have been more suitable in a Canaanite temple than as a celebration of Yahweh's glory—since it is described as 'marqod',[78] the name of the Phoenician deity, Baal Marqod, *lord of the dance*.

---

[77] Many scholars think there were more. Eight is simply the tally of his named wives. It is unclear whether the count of concubines includes Saul's wife Ahinoam and his concubine Rizpah. It does not seem to include Abishag who warmed him in his old age. That Saul's wives—or at least Rizpah, since she was still alive when David came to power—are given to David is clear from God's rebuke delivered through Nathan after David's affair with Bathsheba: *'I gave your master's house to you and your master's wives into your arms. I gave you the house of Israel and Judah, and if that was not enough, I would have given you even more.'* (2 Samuel 12:8[BSB]) David should have married within his own tribe in order to keep the land rights inheritance from becoming confused. He acquired Carmel and the other extensive estates when he married Nabal's widow Abigail. Since Nabal was a Calebite, it seems this territorial acquisition is legitimate. His other personal holdings included Ziklag (given to him by the Philistines), Jerusalem (within the territory of Benjamin) and Rabbah of the Ammonites (perhaps notionally within the territory of Gad). In addition, he may have had property in Hebron, his first capital, and some inheritance in Bethlehem.

Now the Ark had been separated from the Tabernacle since it had been lost in battle with the Philistines. With the destruction of so much of the House of Eli, the Tabernacle had moved from Shiloh to Gibeon. But David, in deciding to move the Ark, did not reunite it with the Tabernacle. Instead he proposed to build a Temple, then shift the Tabernacle and reunite it with the Ark—all in Jerusalem.

This is a political statement, not a spiritual one.

His predecessor Saul had actually moved himself and his capital to Gibeon to be with the Tabernacle.[79] David, however, wanted the move to go the other way—to bring the Tabernacle to himself and his capital.[80] This spiritual power dynamic is so alluring that it remains even to the present day: we are encouraged to invite Jesus into our heart, not to accept His invitation to enter by faith into His heart through the wound in His side and there be born again.[81]

He is to come to us, not we go to Him.

Now there's no question Michal was wrong to despise David. However she was not wrong to call him out. David was wrong to dishonour her father and her family and to dishonour God as well, doubling down on his behaviour by not only refusing

---

78   1 Chronicles 15:29. Since other Hebrew words for *dance* could have been used, the choice of 'marqod' seems a deliberate pointer to the Phoenician deity.

79   He moved from Gibeah to Gibeon.

80   Politically, Gibeon was associated with Saul and his kingdom. Religiously, it was associated with the Tabernacle and all the worship there. David's desire to build a Temple in Jerusalem has overtones of wanting to divest himself entirely of the entwined political and religious associations of Gibeon. That would have been fine if God had asked for it, but since He didn't, the spectre of David's own ambition is inescapable.

81   See: *The Lustral Waters*, the third book in this series.

to repent of his obscene display but by insisting, 'But it was for the Lord!'

How often do we hear today of leaders rationalising similarly? For the sake of the gospel, so they insist, allegations of abuse and misconduct must not be spoken of. It takes courage to confront, but all too often, those who have been abused are muzzled. *It's for the Lord* is the pretext and excuse for demanding silence.

Michal spoke truth to power. David's response to her was dishonouring, insulting and demeaning.[82] He apparently never forgave her because the record says she never had a child, not that

---

[82] It was particularly insensitive, given the strong possibility that Uzzah, the man killed on trying to steady the Ark of the Covenant when it had been in danger of falling, was her nephew. She would therefore have been in mourning. Uzzah's death was the result of David's negligence in applying the statutes of the Torah. As king, he was supposed to have written out the Torah by hand and meditated on it daily. So the responsibility for knowing how to transport the Ark was squarely his. Now Uzzah's father was Abinadab of Gibeah, a hill outside Kiriath Jearim on the border between the territory of Benjamin and Judah. Clearly he was a man of status, since he was assigned to keep the Ark after seventy people from Beth Shemesh died looking into it.

Now one of Saul's sons was named Abinadab. Was the Abinadab who had guardianship of the Ark the same man? We cannot be sure but it seems likely. First, it would be logical for the Ark to be given into the keeping of a prince of the realm. Second, the designation 'of Gibeah' seems a deliberate hint that this household belongs to a member of Saul's family since they originally came from Gibeah (albeit a different one). Now Prince Abinadab was killed at Mount Gilboa during the battle with the Philistines, some years before the removal of the Ark from Kiriath Jearim to Jerusalem. But his house and household may well have endured. Abinadab's son Eleazar had been consecrated to care for the Ark when it first came to Kiriath Jearim. If Abinadab was indeed Saul's son, then Eleazar was a Benjaminite. But if Abinadab was not Saul's son, then he was likely a man of Judah. Either way, he was not a Levite or of the lineage of Aaron.

As for Michal, it must have been heartbreaking to realise that, had David kept his covenant with Jonathan, then the death of her brother Abinadab might have been averted. And if Uzzah was her nephew, then David's ongoing negligence had led to the needless death of Abinadab's son.

she was *barren*. What it tells us is that he never approached her again. She's the only woman in all Scripture described as loving a man. David's betrayal must have run deep.

Indeed by having children with his other wives and spurning Michal, David failed to complete the last of the three tasks that Saul was faced with when he became king. David did no better. He did not reconcile the people of Bethlehem, his hometown, with the people of Gibeah, Michal's hometown. This reconciliation was needed after the civil war that pitted the tribe of Benjamin against all the others and that resulted in a generational feud between Bethlehem and Gibeah.[83] This hostility could have been ended by David, and would have been achieved by a child of his union with Michal.

But David was changed by power. He had his moments of utmost humility but this was not one of them. Now, despite his insistence what he'd done was for the Lord and therefore acceptable, David seems to have been deeply worried by what Michal had said. He'd insulted her father, reminding her that God had chosen to replace Saul with David himself. Now, ironically, dynastic succession was lost to Saul because he'd acted, illegitimately, as a priest. It probably occurred to David to wonder at that very moment whether his sacrifice of burnt offerings and fellowship offerings while dressed in a priest's ephod was acceptable and legitimate, if Saul's was not.

Perhaps, at the end of the day, David's actions were no more righteous or unrighteous than Saul's. Perhaps the judgment of God was the same in both cases. Perhaps David lost the chance of a dynasty issuing from him and ruling over a unified kingdom at this very moment. Saul had a son briefly rule after him; David had

---

83 Jonathan tried to mend the breach between Gibeah and Bethlehem by making covenant with David.

a son rule for a long time after him. But then, both their grandsons were simply tribal heads, even if Rehoboam styled himself 'king'.

Only in Jesus does the righteousness of the House of David, along with the reward of the secure and everlasting covenant that David laid a claim to, make any sense at all.

4.2 Five

Jesus said to her, 'Go, call your husband, and come here.' The woman answered him, 'I have no husband.' Jesus said to her, 'You are right in saying, "I have no husband" for you have had five husbands, and the one you now have is not your husband. What you have said is true.'

John 4:16–18^{ESV}

'What is truth?' retorted Pilate. With this he went out again to the Jews gathered there and said, 'I find no basis for a charge against Him.'

John 18:38^{NIV}

THE NUMBER 'FIVE' COMES TO the forefront in this dialogue between the Samaritan woman and Jesus when He reveals she has had five husbands. And, as we've seen, there are several fives lurking in the background of the conversation:

- Five men who reaffirmed covenant in this location
- Five foreign cities where the Samaritans originated
- Five women who had an encounter at a well that changed their lives
- The letter/number 'hei' for *five* that signifies the breath of God[84]

---

84 5 is the difference in the gematria of the names Abraham and Abram. In Hebrew, only the letter 'hei' is added to Abram to make Abraham.

Now the number *five* is present in the chiastic section at the end of the gospel too and, like these historical *fives*, it is also far from obvious. Pontius Pilate was the fifth Roman governor of Judea who had been appointed after the ethnarch Herod Archelaus[85] was deposed. The last king had been Herod the Great, the father of Archelaus. Moreover, the name Pontius means either *five* or *sea* or *bridge-builder*.

Five will return again in the next chapter when John mentions the number of colonnades at the Pool of Bethesda. Throughout Scripture, it is often associated with groups of women. There were five women who saved the life of Moses at the beginning of the book of Exodus.[86] At the end of the book of Numbers—chiastically placed within the five books of the Torah—another five women appear to successfully petition to inherit land in their own right and set a new legal precedent. These are the daughters of Zelophehad. There are five women mentioned in the genealogy of Jesus in Matthew's gospel,[87] although clearly there have to have been a lot more than that! There are five women designated as prophets in the Hebrew Scriptures, though once again, there were clearly more than that.[88] There are five barren women

---

85 Archelaus was the son of Herod's wife Malthace who was a Samaritan. Herod the Great himself was an Idumean, a descendant of Esau.

86 Four of the five are named in Exodus itself and the fifth one, Pharaoh's daughter, is named in Chronicles. The named women are the midwives, Shiphrah and Puah; Miriam, the sister of Moses, and Jochebed, his mother. The daughter of Pharaoh remains unnamed in Exodus, but her name is revealed as Bithiah in 1 Chronicles 4:17. The five women at the end of Numbers are Mahlah, Tirzah, Hoglah, Milkah and Noah—Zelophehad's daughters.

87 Tamar, Rahab, Ruth, Uriah's wife and Mary, mother of Jesus. 'Uriah's wife' is a strange expression but perhaps it suggests that, like the other women preceding her in the list, she was a foreigner. Uriah was famously a Hittite.

88 Miriam, Deborah, Huldah, Noadiah and 'the prophetess' who was married to Isaiah.

mentioned too.[89] There may have been five women at the death and resurrection of Jesus.[90]

The number five is often said to symbolise *grace*[91] or unmerited *favour*.

Now in addition to the hidden fives in the name Pontius—as well as his position as the fifth governor—that connect his dialogue with Jesus to that of the woman, both sections have a theme of *truth*. Jesus declares that what the woman has said is true—regardless of how nuanced that truth might have been. And Pilate famously queries, *'What is truth?'* when Truth was standing right in front of him, under judgment.

---

89   Sarah, Rebekah, Rachel, Hannah and the wife of Manoah who was also the mother of Samson. Michal, as we've seen, is not described as barren but as childless.

90   The various descriptions by the gospel writers are not clear and we can only conclude there were somewhere between four and seven. For more on this motif of 'five women' in Scripture, see: Anne Hamilton, Donna Ho, Natalie Tensen, *As Exceptional as Sapphires: The Mother's Blessing and God's Favour Towards Women III*, Armour Books, 2021

91   This widely disseminated idea is based on the work of EW Bullinger who listed various fives and fifths in Scripture. Some, but by no means all, of these examples have a theme of grace. See, for example: friendsofsabbath.org/Further_Research/Bible/number_in_scripture/five.htm (accessed 11 November 2024) *Grace* itself has a gematria of 68, as does *life* and *wisdom* as well as *prophetess*, *'Yah is great'*, *'I will extol him'*, *despise* and *prostitute*. Like names—which always have both a positive and a negative choice encoded in them—numbers have both positive and negative spiritual connotations. Now, while Bullinger claimed that five was the number of *grace*, the reasoning behind his deduction is not in my view particularly solid or unassailable. In *Numbers in Scripture*, he points out that there are 'five great mysteries: Father, Son, Spirit, Creation and Redemption… and five therefore is the number of GRACE.' However, we could suggest that there are three great mysteries: Trinity, Creation and Redemption—what then? Or we could add the final judgment to the mysteries—what then for the count and therefore for the symbolism of five as *grace*? Five, I believe, better symbolises the *breath of the Spirit* as indicated by the Hebrew letter, 'hei', for *breath*.

Was that a cynical question? Was it distrustful of people's motives? Or suspicious of their own self-awareness? Did he really want to know or was it just a bit of shrugging rhetoric?

Pilate was probably not asking in a philosophical sense but as a judge who had to weigh the veracity of so many accusers and accused brought before him. He'd know the practical complexities of extricating the truth from hostile or reluctant witnesses. However, as a philosophical construct in antiquity, 'aletheia', *truth*, was contrasted with 'doxa', *public opinion*. Literally, 'aletheia' was a combination of 'a-', *not*, and '-lethe', *forgetful*. However it was usually understood as *revealing, unveiling* or *disclosure*.

All of these shades of meaning are built into both scenes. And there is still another as well: the Hebraic concept of truth. For the Jews, 'truth is as much encounter as it is proposition.'[92] Jesus is in the process of unveiling Himself as the Messiah to the woman, and as a divine king to Pilate. He encourages each to hold the line against the pressure of public opinion and make a stand for what each of them knows, by the whispering breath of the Holy Spirit, to be true. He is urging them not to be forgetful or fearful, and so to dismiss truth as relative, not absolute.

Pilate in fact declares Jesus to be the King of the Jews in the inscription nailed to the Cross. He thus indicates to the Jewish leaders precisely what he thinks about the truthfulness of their statement, *'We have no king but Caesar.'*[93] Now once again, the number five appears—this time in relation to the inscription. The Greek word, 'graphō', *to write*, is used five times in the preparation and the protest over its wording.[94]

---

92   Marvin R Wilson, *Our Father Abraham: Jewish Roots of the Christian Faith*, Eerdmans Publishing 1989
93   John 19:15[NIV]
94   John 19:19–22

Pilate certainly tried to pronounce an ethical, rather than arbitrary, judgment. *'I find no basis for a charge against Him.'* Truth is essential to integrity. Moreover, the giving of freedom would have been integral to Pilate's own personal identity, since *freeman* is the most likely meaning of 'pilate'. The name is thought to derive from 'pileus' or 'pilos', a close-fitting brimless felt cap placed on a slave's head on being set free. These caps were generally conical, but others were skullcaps similar to the kippah worn today by orthodox Jews.[95] For the Jewish people, the concept of *covering* is intimately connected with *atonement* and here we see Jesus symbolically losing the covering of Roman law as His ultimate act of atonement draws closer.

Pilate's integrity was compromised by his insecurity—a weakness his opponents knew just how to exploit. Perhaps, in fact, it wasn't Pilate's personal weakness they were manipulating but a weakness of the entire empire. For many years during the reign of Tiberius, Rome was ruled by the tyrannical and murderous administrator Sejanus who had consolidated power in his hands. The emperor had retired to Capri, disillusioned and paranoid after the death of his son, Drusus. Pilate was aware that the slightest accusation, true or false, from the Jewish leaders to Sejanus would have potentially fatal consequences.[96]

Now the other possible answer to Pilate's question, *'What is truth?'*—apart of course from Jesus Himself as Truth incarnate—is *'Scripture'*. And much as I am loath to employ gematria if I can possibly avoid it, because it's so easy to slide into the hidden

---

[95] The Jews have not always worn the kippah. From the 12–17th centuries, the Jews of Europe wore a pointed version called the 'pileus cornutus'.

[96] It's difficult to be sure in what year the trial of Jesus occurred, but assuming the dating specified in *The Summoning of Time* is correct, then Pilate would have been threatened by the Jewish leaders on 4 or 5 April in 30 AD, the last year of Sejanus' rule.

knowledge of Gnosticism, there's also no doubt it was in common usage in antiquity. That usage includes the Bible.

Now the gematria of 'Mah emeth?', the Hebrew phrase for *'What is truth?'* is 486 and so is 'grammata', one of the possible Greek alternatives for *epistle, writing* or *Scripture*. For many Jews, this match of numbers would not have been coincidental but an indication of God's design in the patterning of word and number.

4.3 Bridge-builders

'I find no basis for a charge against Him.'

John 18:38^{NIV}

With these words, Pilate declares Jesus innocent of the accusations made against Him, and judges Him not guilty and blameless. He also tries to bring about an acquittal. Pilate may not be saying Jesus is righteous but he's implying it.

The dialogue between them to this point has revolved around *kingship* but now we have an extra element to factor in: *righteousness*.

Perhaps in regard to his combination we might think of David who, in the eulogy he wrote for himself just before he died, said:

> *If my house were not right with God, surely He would not have made with me an everlasting covenant, arranged and secured in every part; surely He would not bring to fruition my salvation and grant me my every desire.*
>
> 2 Samuel 23:5^{NIV}

More than a little reverse engineering is present in these words. David basically claimed not just righteous rule for himself but also for his dynasty *because* God favoured him. This is salvation by works, not by grace. The failure to recognise God's grace is unmerited means that David felt justified in saying he must have been just and blameless, otherwise God would not have rewarded, blessed and saved him.

A better choice than David is Melchizedek, king of Salem,[97] whose name means *king of righteousness*. The conflict between Pilate and the Jewish leaders was not just about kingship but about priesthood.

Pontius can mean not only *five* but *bridge-builder*. The creation of bridges was considered a sacred art and a 'pontifex', *bridge-builder*, was considered to have divine powers. Over time in the Roman republic and later empire, 'pontifex' come to mean much more than *bridge-builder*, it came to mean *priest*—the mediator or the bridge between humanity and the gods.

Now the 'pontifex maximus' was the chief priest. The 'pontifex maximus' in Rome was equivalent to the high priest, Caiaphas, in Jerusalem. It was the most powerful office in the state religion of ancient Rome but it was not the highest ranking. In fact, it was fifth in the sacred order.[98] It directed the College of Pontiffs, a description that was used from the third century to describe

---

[97] Salem is usually considered to be the same as Jerusalem. However there is a Salim (also spelled Salem and Shalem) just three kilometres (two miles) east of Jacob's Well. *'And Jacob came to Shalem, a city of Shechem, which is in the land of Canaan, when he came from Padanaram; and pitched his tent before the city.'* (Genesis 33:18[KJV]) More modern translations simply say Jacob came *safely* to the city of Shechem and do not regard the word 'salem' as a proper name. The proximity of the village of Salim to modern Nablus (ancient Shechem) is simply regarded as a remarkable coincidence.

However, if the Salem ruled by Melchizedek was in the area of Shechem, then Abraham would have known him from his earliest journey through the land when he stopped nearby to build that first altar. Perhaps the oracle tree of the Oaks of Moreh was part of Melchizedek's land. Moreover, this might be the same place as the Salim that John the Baptiser moved to, when he relocated from Bethany-beyond-the-Jordan.

[98] After Rex Sacrorum, Flamen Dialis, Flamen Martialis, and Flamen Quirinalis.

bishops of the church and still used by the Vatican as an official papal title.

Caesar Augustus adopted the title of 'pontifex maximus' thus becoming a priest-emperor. Pilate, as the representative of Augustus' successor Tiberius, and also as a governor whose name resounds with aspects of that fifth level of the state cult of priesthood, brings to the confrontation with the Jewish leaders far more than a political clash. His altercation with the chief priests is a collision between the religion of Rome and that of the Jerusalem.

Did they know they were actually fighting over the legitimacy of Jesus as the priest-king of Jerusalem? I suspect Annas and Caiaphas had an inkling and that's why they were so threatened.

Before Herod's lavish refurbishment of the Temple, the high priests had been chosen by lot from amongst the descendants of Aaron and remained in that position for life. Herod however wanted to stem the political power they wielded, so he appointed the holder of the office himself. Then the wealthy Sadducee, Annas, bought the position from the Roman governor. He was the first high priest of the new Roman province of Judea. Although he was deposed after nine years and there was a rapid turnover of three high priests in the next three years, his son-in-law Caiaphas was eventually appointed to the role and held the office for 18 years. Even after his dismissal and throughout the turbulent years when several priestly families were vying for political control, Annas maintained a mafia-like grip on the flow of wealth into his family's coffers. His family operated four booths on the Mount of Olives, specialising in the sale of sacrificial offerings at inflated prices. In addition, in the month before the Passover, money-changers were stationed in the 'bazaars of the sons of Annas' in the Temple courtyard to facilitate the collection of the Temple tax.[99] They traded ordinary currency for the special half-shekel at an outrageous mark-up. By choosing a silver coin from Tyre with a blasphemous image on it as the only legitimate way to pay the tax, they tied the people up in a spiritual double bind: the people could ignore the tax and disobey a command of God regarding the atonement or they could pay it and break the commandment about graven images. In addition to this spiritual bondage, the family of Annas refused to pay tithes on their sales, extorted money, and stole funds intended to support priests who had no other income.

The corruption ran deep and the people were looking forward to the overthrow of the violence, fraud, bribery and exploitation. They were watching out eagerly for the coming of not just one Messiah, but three different ones:

- the Son of David, the royal Messiah
- the Son of Joseph, the war Messiah
- the priest of the order of Melchizedek, the priestly Messiah

This long tradition—based on an understanding of the four craftsmen[100] in the vision of Zechariah—spoke of a descendant of the tribe of Judah as the royal Messiah, a descendant of the tribe of Joseph as the war Messiah, and a non-Levite as the priestly Messiah. In fact, since David had appointed his sons as priests, there was a chance that two of the positions could be combined.

No one was expecting them all to be united in one person.

Straight after the episode of David's dance before the Ark of the Covenant, God promised him there'd always be one of his descendants on the throne. David clearly saw it as reassurance

---

99 See: ourrabbijesus.com/articles/new-light-on-jesus-last-week-part-i/ (accessed 11 November 2024)

100 Zechariah 1:20

that his dynasty was secure. And, quite frankly, he'd have needed that reassurance considering his words to Michal:

> *I was dancing before the Lord, who chose me above your father and all his family! He appointed me as the leader of Israel, the people of the Lord, so I celebrate before the Lord.*
>
> 2 Samuel 6:21^{NLT}

After David had put Michal back in her place and insulted her father and his sons, including his blood-brother Jonathan, it might have dawned on him that there was a singular reason why Saul was denied a dynasty—and that was because he'd acted like a priest. Perhaps it then occurred to David that wearing a linen ephod and sacrificing a bull and a calf every six steps was acting just like a priest too. And if that thought did cross his mind, he'd have been worried. Would God judge Saul for offering sacrifices without priestly authority, and not similarly judge David? Surely God was fair and just. If doubts didn't assail David at this point, then power had already hugely corrupted him.

God, however, reassured him through the prophet Nathan.

> *'Your house and your kingdom will endure forever before Me; your throne will be established forever.'*
>
> 2 Samuel 7:16^{NIV}

But this word from God did not mean what David thought it did. Merely one generation along the track beyond him, the throne of his house was diminished to the point where it was basically tribal headship, not the rulership of a unified brotherhood of clans. From an earthly perspective, David's kingdom lasted just as long as Saul's did, and no longer. A single king followed the head of the house, and thereafter the leadership reverted to rule over one main tribe. The kingdom of David's grandson Rehoboam was curtailed to the territory of Judah and its capital, Jerusalem, situated in the tribal allotment of Benjamin. Sure, it had a glorious Temple but it was attended only by the tribe of Judah.[101] And, sure, there were 21 rulers of David's line before the exile to Babylon but afterwards the kingship disappeared for centuries. The Greeks ruled and, when they were overthrown, the Hasmonean dynasty come from a priestly family, not the descendants of David. Herod was an Idumean, a descendant of Esau and not even Jewish.

Therefore God's promise to David makes no sense whatsoever in the light of history. It is unconditional only when applied to Jesus. In the natural course of events, that divine pledge was entirely swept away within a few decades. Indeed Psalm 89 begins by reciting God's oath to David before launching into a grief-stricken lament and flatly accusing God of promise-breaking.[102]

Only in Jesus is the eternal throne an unassailable reality.

David's action in appointing his sons as priests[103] is so extraordinary it seems almost inconceivable that we don't get to hear why. It's such a major break with Levitical norms we should surely hear of some revelation from God to justify it. But there's nothing.

---

101 Later also by Benjamin.

102 After laying out God's promises to David and proclaiming God's faithfulness, the psalm suddenly backflips: *'But You have rejected, You have spurned, You have been very angry with Your anointed one. You have renounced the covenant with Your servant and have defiled his crown in the dust. You have broken through all his walls and reduced his strongholds to ruins. All who pass by have plundered him; he has become the scorn of his neighbours. You have exalted the right hand of his foes; You have made all his enemies rejoice. Indeed, You have turned back the edge of his sword and have not supported him in battle. You have put an end to his splendour and cast his throne to the ground. You have cut short the days of his youth; You have covered him with a mantle of shame. How long, Lord? Will You hide yourself forever?'* (Psalm 89:38–46[NIV])

103 2 Samuel 8:18

The only possible hint we get is in Psalm 110, often tag-lined *'Of David'* but just as possibly being *'To David'*.[104]

> *The Lord has sworn and will not change His mind:*
> *'You are a priest forever, in the order of Melchizedek.'*
>
> Psalm 110:4[NIV]

In rabbinic understanding, this is not a song *by David* but a short choir piece sung by the Levites *to David* celebrating his unique election to a priest-king role. David, apparently, looked for legitimacy for his behaviour in acting as a priest and appointing his sons as priests by appealing to the tradition of Melchizedek, priest-king of Salem. We have no indication God approved of this; on the contrary, since the priesthood of Jesus according to the order of Melchizedek is inviolable, permanent, unchangeable, exclusive, untransferable and without successor,[105] it seems He did not.

We tend to think David's actions must have been given a tick by God because the psalm is Messianic prophecy. Surely, many of us ponder to ourselves, David couldn't possibly have been so accurate if he wasn't in alignment with God's purposes. But this is like saying, 'The end justifies the means.' It's like admitting that we don't believe God can bring good out of the most harrowing evil or that He won't bring a prophecy to pass despite the most dubious possible motives in proclaiming it. The world today is full of prophets and priests prostituting their gift for gain, but God does not snatch back the gift. It wouldn't be a gift if He did.

He tells us to recognise His followers by their fruit, not their gifts.

---

104 Either translation is valid.
105 See: the meaning of the Greek word 'aparabatos' in Hebrews 7:24 at biblehub.com/greek/531.htm (accessed 21 November 2024)

So then, what is the fruit of David's life? How did he end up? Virtually alone,[106] afraid of God,[107] complicit with the satan[108] and intent on vengeance.[109]

Jesus, the one and only true priest-king of the order of Melchizedek,[110] is the bridge-builder to God. Neither the Roman priesthood or the Jewish priesthood recognised Him, even as they scuffled for power and scrabbled to dominate each other. But the one who did recognise Him was the woman of Samaria. He built the bridge but she brought the citizens of her town to come and pass over it.

---

106   1 Kings 1:1–4. Clearly none of his wives are there.

107   1 Chronicles 21:29–30

108   1 Chronicles 21:1

109   See 1 Kings 2:5–9 for his instructions to Solomon about those who irritated him in life and therefore need to be put to death. David rewards Joab's ruthless and often obsessive loyalty with execution. Perhaps he viewed Joab in the same way as Saul had once viewed David—as a threat to his dynasty and Solomon in particular. See also his torture of the Ammonites: strateias.org/torture.htm (accessed 12 August 2024)

110   No one else qualifies. Despite this, a priesthood of the order of Melchizedek exists within both in the Mormon Church and Freemasonry, as well as some prophetic groups. However, given the unique, exclusive, non-transferable and inviolable nature of the role that, according to Hebrews 7:24, admits of no successor, this is at best a mistaken understanding. So where does that leave us in the priesthood of all believers? Rather than being in the order of Melchizedek, it would seem we are part of a restored and extended priesthood. Before the Levites of the line of Aaron were given the role of priests for the nation of Israel, every male was a priest in his own household. Every firstborn son was a priest for the wider family. That was the structure of the original priesthood until the sin of the golden calf. Afterwards, men lost this privilege and it was given to the Levites. The restored priesthood, however, is different. It extends even beyond firstborn and beyond males to women as well.

4.4 Call Your Husband

Jesus said to her, 'Go, call your husband, and come here.'

John 4:16^{ESV}

IN THE OLD LANGUAGE, He might have said, 'Call your baal.' For 'baal' means *husband, lord, master, owner*. There's a certain ambiguity in that command of Jesus for it could have meant anyone from her employer to the godling she worshipped. The citizens of the five cities who were transplanted into the Samaritan heartland by the Assyrians each had their own godling—their own 'baal'— Succoth-benoth, Nergal, Ashima, Nihbaz and Tartak. To begin with, those settlers worshipped these gods before realising the land was hostile to them and turning to Yahweh. Perhaps Jesus was alluding to these five deities in His comment: perhaps He was pointing out that the people had never truly divested themselves of the five city-lords they'd venerated in the east, and as a result, they had never genuinely attached themselves to the sixth— Yahweh Himself. Their loyalties were divided, their worship was double-minded, their covenants were tainted.

Nor should we forget in this mix the goddess-of-sovereignty motif that existed across so many cultures and involved meeting strange women at wells. The Jews didn't have a goddess of sovereignty, since their sole allegiance was—at least in theory—given to Yahweh.

But, in practice, lingering aspects of that pagan idea floated around the royal women. And, of course, for the Canaanites, the goddess of sovereignty—the one with the right to decide who should succeed to the kingship—was Anat.[111]

It's unclear exactly what role the royal women of Israel had in determining the kingship, but it is nonetheless clear that a liaison with one of them constituted a potential claim on the throne. Adonijah, the older half-brother of Solomon—the prince who saw himself as the natural successor to David and who had set himself up as king even as his father was dying—asked Bathsheba to petition King Solomon on his behalf to allow him to marry Abishag. She was the young girl who'd slept with David to keep him warm in his last days. Apparently, none of his wives or concubines were up to the task. Now David hadn't had sexual relations with Abishag but obviously just being in his bed gave her a status similar to a wife. Solomon was incandescent with fury on hearing Adonijah's request. He reacted violently, saying:

> *You might as well ask me to give him the kingdom!*
>
> 1 Kings 2:22^{NLT}

He then ordered the immediate execution of Adonijah.

That seems like a massive overreaction—yet there are hints elsewhere that sleeping with a king's wife, even if she were a widow, was considered treasonous. It might not be the full goddess-of-sovereignty notion but it's definitely partaking of very similar thinking.

---

[111] It was not only the Canaanites who believed this. Rameses the Great of Egypt, for example, regularly calls her the Mistress or Lady of Heaven in the context of claiming Anat's support in battle and legitimation of his right to 'universal' rule. See: Karel van der Toorn, Bob Becking, Pieter Willem van der Horst, *Dictionary of Deities and Demons in the Bible*, Wm. B. Eerdmans Publishing, 1999

At one time there were two kings in Israel—Ish-bosheth, the son of Saul, who had the loyalty of most of the tribes, and David who had the backing of the men of Judah. The catalyst for a shift in allegiance from Ish-bosheth to David was a royal woman. Ish-bosheth had a falling out with Abner, the commander-in-chief of his armies. Ish-bosheth had confronted Abner over the fact he was sleeping with Saul's concubine, Rizpah. The altercation was so fierce that Abner switched sides. He sent messengers to David, proposing a covenant between them. David's response was that he'd agree only if he got his wife Michal back. She'd remarried—and her new husband deeply loved her. It wasn't as if David was lonely for female company—he had at least two other wives at this stage and was apparently in the process of acquiring four more, including the daughter of Talmai, the king of Geshur, *the land of bridges*, on the north-eastern shore of the Sea of Galilee.

Michal, however, was David's first wife—and now that he was contending for the kingship with Ish-bosheth, it was possible her remarriage gave a stranger a claim on the throne. Michal was the bargaining chip in the transfer of power to David. She herself was powerless but her position granted power to the men who, one after another, controlled her life.

Now, if indeed Jesus is dealing with the episode of David's shameless dancing in this meeting with the Samaritan woman, then she must represent Michal in some way. The woman's five marriages, whether they ended in death or divorce, represent a long and complex period of pain and abandonment. Michal's marital situation, while different, was also a long and complex period of pain and abandonment.

So in healing this ancient wound involving Michal's pain, powerlessness, sense of abandonment and no doubt rejection as well as David's shamelessness and unforgiveness, Jesus had to tread a fine line. He had to approach the line that society considers shameless without actually crossing it, He had to give the woman agency, and He also had to accept her as she was. In addition, He had to raise a covenant with her and then keep His word: to be, as the Samaritans thought of themselves, a 'keeper' of divine law.

All of these things are present in His interaction with her. She doesn't just represent the land, she isn't just a representative of, and an antitype to, the pagan goddess of sovereignty, she also embodies the royal women of the past who were bartered for power and prestige.

4.5 Mastering Kingdoms

Now you might think I stretched the story a bit too fair by suggesting that the Samaritan woman represents Michal. However, Michal's name is significant in this regard. It is often said to be a variation on Michael, *who is like the Lord?*, the name of the angelic prince who is the guardian of Israel.

However, Michal is spelled the same way in Hebrew as 'mikal', *a brook* or *streamlet*, thus reminding us of 'living water' as sourced in a *running stream*. Her name is also spelled the same way as Mekal, the name of the patron deity of Beit She'an, the city where the bodies of Saul and those of his sons who were slain in battle were affixed to the walls. Beit She'an eventually became Scythopolis—the only city of the ten towns of Decapolis on the west bank of the Jordan. Jesus would have passed through Scythopolis on His way to Jerusalem from Galilee. In the first century, it had a massive Temple to either Herakles or Dionysius and, as outlined in *The Summoning of Time*, John showed how Jesus had the victory over both of these deities in the second chapter of his gospel.

Now He is building up to an even greater conquest: that over Mekal, also known as Resheph, the antlered gatekeeper of the underworld and the spiritual patron of Shechem. This triumph is not outlined in the fourth chapter, but it will be by the end of the story about Lazarus. The story of the Samaritan woman is backgrounded by the town's ancient worship of Mekal-Resheph. Furthermore it is the lynchpin between the second chapter and the eleventh involving Mary, Martha and Lazarus—and the defeat of the gods of Beit-She'an.

Besides being evocative of living water, Michal's name is also a rhyme for 'machol', a *twisting, whirling dance*. Our modern tendency is to overlook poetry as a significant component of identity, focussing only on the etymological meaning of a name. This ignores the relationship between the calling into our destiny and the poetry wrought into our character and identity:

> *For we are His workmanship* [Greek: POETRY], *created in Christ Jesus for good works, which God prepared beforehand that we should walk in them.*
>
> Ephesians 2:10^{NKJV}

David's dance defiled Michal's identity. And, as previously noted, by not fathering a child of the marriage, he failed in completing the third task in the great assignment of healing the nation—he did not bring about reconciliation between the people of Bethlehem and the people of Gibeah.

He may have mastered kingdoms, been the 'baal baalim' in one sense, but he did not master his own household or his attitude. The phrase *'mastered kingdoms'* was used by the Jewish historian Josephus to describe David. William Barclay picks up on the expression in his translation of the rollcall of faith in Hebrews:

> *And what more shall I say? Time will fail me if I try to recount the story of Gideon, of Barak, of Samson, or Jephthah, of David. of Samuel and of the prophets, men who, through faith, mastered kingdoms, did righteousness, obtained promises, shut the mouths of lions, quenched the power of fire, escaped the edge of the sword. from weakness*

were made strong, showed themselves strong in warfare, routed the ranks of aliens.[112]

Hebrews 11:32-34

Immediately after *'mastering kingdoms'* comes *'did righteousness'*, the description of David towards all his subjects in 2 Samuel 8:15, just before the chronicler mentions he appointed his sons as priests, relates the story of his kindness to Mephibosheth and then calls the statement about righteousness into question by exposing his relationship with Bathsheba.

The honour Jesus shows to women throughout His life contrasts with that of the men who mistreated and dishonoured them. In His recapitulation of history at Shechem, in His reworking of the stories, His rejigging of the plotlines, His repair of faithlines and ancient abuses, He deals with more than one bygone tragedy involving various women. There's not just Michal, there's also Hagar, and also the women who were sent away in the time of Ezra and Nehemiah.

In the parallel story—the trial before Pilate—He deals the sacrifice of two sons and five grandsons of Saul: the children of Rizpah, Saul's concubine, and of Merab, Saul's daughter. The echoes of the Gibeonites' statement to David, *'It is not for us to execute anyone in Israel,'* are eerie and harrowing, and the congruence between David and Pilate is plain.

David is not blameless in handing over the sons of Saul to the Gibeonites. He's just like Pilate. The parallel also indicates that the chief priests who condemned Jesus had the same contempt for God that the Gibeonites had. They had been asked by David

---

112 Translated: *The Letter to the Hebrews, The Daily Study Bible Revised Edition*, The St Andrews Press, Edinburgh, 1976

to bless the Lord's inheritance, instead they cursed the land by leaving the bodies unburied. They were as wily as their Canaanite ancestors—deceiving the leader of the nation and leaving him powerless to enforce justice in the face of their duplicity.

The chief priests, for all their pretensions, were no better than these despised labourers—the hewers of wood and drawers of water who served the Levites of old. Significantly Jesus is not compared to David in this recapitulation but to the sons of Saul. In the summing up of the Lord's work of redemption, that's what the equation says:

- David corresponds to Pilate
- The chief priests correspond to the Gibeonites
- Jesus corresponds to the sons of Saul.

Jesus might be the long-anticipated king in the line of David but He is not a king in the mould of David. He is instead the master who is also the servant.

4.6 Prophet You Are

> *The woman said to Him, 'Sir, I perceive that You are a prophet. Our fathers worshipped on this mountain, but You say that in Jerusalem is the place where people ought to worship.'*
>
> *Jesus said to her, 'Woman, believe Me, the hour is coming when neither on this mountain nor in Jerusalem will you worship the Father.'*
>
> John 4:19–21[ESV]

IN YODA-LIKE SPEECH, the Samaritan woman replies to Jesus' revelation about her five husbands with the statement, 'Prophet You are.'[113] That's the way it comes out in Greek and, although most translations render it as 'a *prophet*', it's more likely to be 'THE *prophet*'. Unlike the Jews with their Tanakh (comprised of the Law, Prophets and Writings), the Samaritans had only the Law, the Torah. So the woman wouldn't have been thinking of someone like Isaiah or Ezekiel, Daniel or Hosea; she would have had only one prophet in mind—Moses. No one else.

---

113 See: cmj-usa.org/blog/prophet-moses-offers-water-israelite (accessed 11 November 2024)

In first century Jewish tradition, one of the ways it was anticipated the Messiah would be able to recognised was that He'd be able to cast out demons specialising in deafness and dumbness.[114] However, in the Samaritan tradition, the 'Taheb' or Restorer would make Himself known by His possession of supernatural knowledge. The Taheb was the Samaritan equivalent of the Messiah and was understood to be the prophet that Moses had promised when he said:

> *The Lord your God will raise up for you a prophet like me from among you, from your fellow Israelites. You must listen to him.*
>
> Deuteronomy 18:15[NIV]

This prophet-like-Moses would naturally do Moses-like things, such as providing water for those suffering thirst. So it was natural for the woman to put two and two together—supernatural knowledge, the offer of water, the language of gift—and conclude that the Taheb had come.[115]

Some commentators think she was desperately attempting to deflect the conversation away from her lifestyle and previous marriages. Perhaps, but not necessarily. She may well have been hit by the astonishing revelation that the man talking to her is none other than the Taheb. But there's a truly unexpected problem: He's *Jewish!*

---

[114] Jewish exorcists relied on their ability to command ungodly spirits to reveal their names for the exercise of their ministry. On discovering the name, they would then use the power of the name to evict the demonic tenant in a person. However, it was not possible for a person who couldn't hear or speak to respond to such a command. It was so far beyond the ability of the exorcists to remove such spirits it came to be a widespread expectation that only the Messiah could do it. Hence the buzz of excitement by the witnesses, as in Matthew 9:32–33.

[115] See: cmj-usa.org/blog/prophet-moses-offers-water-israelite (accessed 11 November 2024)

The woman, after all, has changed her language. She'd begun by calling Jesus, 'You, a Jew,' then she'd very politely and deferentially called Him, 'Sir'—in Greek, 'kyrie', *lord, master, authority*—before proclaiming Him as 'Prophet'. That, within her cultural understanding, was basically stating He was like Moses, the first deliverer, the original messiah. Just as Nathanael earlier had declared Jesus to be the 'Son of God, the king of Israel', and just as Simon Peter later proclaimed Jesus to be the Messiah through the inspiration of the Father, so the Samaritan woman has been visited by Spirit and Truth and recognised Jesus as the promised Restorer.

This announcement of Jesus as 'Prophet' links back to the previous chapter and its chiastic match which together reveal that Nicodemus is the inheritor of Moses' mantle. In every way, however, this story is a contrast with that of Nicodemus. He's a Jew, she's a Samaritan; he's a man, she's a woman; he's high-class, she's low-class; he's famous, she's nameless; he's privileged, she's underprivileged; he's wealthy, she's humble; he comes by night, she comes by day; he doesn't understand, she gets it; he leaves confused, she leaves enlightened.[116]

Now the immediate dilemma the woman faced as it dawned on her that the Restorer had come was how to share the exciting news when, absolutely unthinkably, He had turned out to be a Jew. Did this mean that she and her fellow-citizens were going to have to abandon their worship on Mount Gerizim and go instead to the Temple in Jerusalem? What would she tell her people? How could she explain it? She put the problem to Jesus straight up:

> 'Our fathers worshipped on this mountain, but You say that in Jerusalem is the place where people ought to worship.'
>
> John 4:20[ESV]

---

116 See: ministrymatters.com/all/entry/741/the-samaritan-woman-and-nicodemus (accessed 11 November 2024)

There is no simple and easy answer to this question. In 2 Samuel 7:5–7, God made it perfectly clear to David that He'd never asked for a Temple and that it was appropriate for Him to dwell in a tent and move from place to place amongst the people. The corresponding passage in 1 Chronicles is even more blunt:

> *You are not the one to build Me a house to dwell in.*
>
> 1 Chronicles 17:4^{NIV}

Nonetheless, having advised against it, God permits the construction to go ahead. It was a situation very much like the institution of kingship itself: God made it clear He was completely against it as it was a rejection of Himself and was simply motivated by a desire to be like other nations. However, having permitted the people to have the kings they wanted, He blessed those who were elevated to the throne. On the surface, David appears to have wanted a Temple for the right reasons: shouldn't God have a better residence than the king? But perhaps his unconscious thought was also to be like other nations and to make a political statement through an imposing edifice. It's one thing to have a city named after you, another entirely to leave a legacy that would be forever named 'David's Temple'.[117]

The way the Temple was paid for reveals its heart-motivation. By the time of Solomon, the building of the Temple had become an

---

[117] It's a curious thing that, in Israel, once the time of the kings arrived, women's names become erased as the names of the kings become ever more prominent. Further with regard to names, there is no longer the 'Tabernacle of God' but instead 'the Temple' that, over time, became 'Solomon's Temple' and 'Herod's Temple', along with the 'Tabernacle of David'. In other nations, we hear of Temple of Artemis or the Temple of Jupiter or the Temple of Rimmon and so on—sanctuaries named for the deity, not for the king who ordered the building. Now, on the one hand, we're right to continue the long tradition of naming these buildings after men. It was never Yahweh's desire to have a Temple for Himself—it was David's and Solomon's and Herod's aspirations. Yet on the other hand, we're entirely wrong because the name glorifies a man, not the One the Temple was built to honour.

excuse for vicious taxation and slave labour. The Tabernacle had been constructed and furnished by freewill offerings and voluntary contributions. It was founded on gratitude and native creativity, while the Temple was built on cruelty and foreign expertise. Even so, despite all the issues, God descended in a cloud of glory at the dedication of the Temple—regardless of His expressed desire not to have it in the first place.

In addition to the abuse that accompanied its construction, it was built on a Jebusite threshing floor—and thus its foundation was a place of divination and communication with the godlings of the Canaanite pantheon. Some of the prophets were surprisingly anti-Temple. Many insisted that God was less interested in sacrifice than in justice, mercy, humility and compassion towards the poor. But some went even further in their denunciation. Ezekiel roundly condemned Jerusalem:

> *Then the word of the Lord came to me, saying, 'Son of man, make known to Jerusalem her abominations and say, "Thus says the Lord God to Jerusalem, 'Your origin and your birth are from the land of the Canaanite, your father was an Amorite and your mother a Hittite.'"'*
>
> Ezekiel 16:1–3^{NASB}

This sentiment—*even your beginnings are corrupt*—is brought out in the famous passage of the prophet Isaiah:

> *Behold, I lay in Zion a stone for a foundation, a tried stone, a precious cornerstone, a sure foundation; whoever believes will not act hastily.*
>
> Isaiah 28:16^{NKJV}

God is speaking in this verse about removing the defilement over the city and laying an entirely new foundation for the Temple—Jesus Himself. The only reason a new foundation is needed is if there's something wrong with the original.

There is no greater denunciation of the Temple in Scripture than that by Jeremiah.

> *Do not trust in deceptive words and say, 'This is the temple of the Lord, the temple of the Lord, the temple of the Lord!'...*
> *'Has this house, which bears My Name, become a den of robbers to you? But I have been watching! declares the Lord. Go now to the place in Shiloh where I first made a dwelling for My Name, and see what I did to it because of the wickedness of My people Israel. While you were doing all these things, declares the Lord, I spoke to you again and again, but you did not listen; I called you, but you did not answer. Therefore, what I did to Shiloh I will now do to the house that bears My Name, the temple you trust in, the place I gave to you and your ancestors.'*
>
> Jeremiah 7:4;11–14[NIV]

The Temple in Jerusalem is no more sacred than the Tabernacle at Shiloh. It's no better. The mountain is irrelevant. The question the woman put to Jesus is wrong in and of itself. It's not a matter of which one is right and which wrong—they are as right and as wrong as each other. Both are distractions from the truth:

> *Jesus said to her, 'Woman, believe Me, the hour is coming when neither on this mountain nor in Jerusalem will you worship the Father.'*
>
> John 4:21[ESV]

As John revealed in his first chapter, the Word became flesh and came to tabernacle in the midst of humanity.[118] That was what God tried to tell David: I'm meant to be moving amongst

---

[118] 'And the Word became flesh and dwelt among us, and we beheld His glory, the glory as of the only begotten of the Father, full of grace and truth.' John 1:14[ESV] The word *'dwelt'* here means *to live in a tent* or *to tabernacle.*

My people, not locked up in a house. My throne is not meant to be in Jerusalem or Shechem but in the hearts and minds of My people.[119]

Indeed, Jesus wants to take up His throne in every heart, and for us to crown Him there as Lord of all, Master of all creation, Saviour of the World, and as Husband and Bridegroom of His worshipping church.

---

119 Stephen, the first martyr, testified to this when he said: *'David found favour in God's sight, and asked that he might find a dwelling place for the house of Jacob. But it was Solomon who built a house for Him. However, the Most High does not dwell in houses made by human hands.'* Acts 7:46–48[NASB]

4.7 Tradition, Tradition

> *But it is your custom for me to release to you one prisoner at the time of the Passover. Do you want me to release 'the king of the Jews'?*
>
> John 18:39^{NIV}

IN CONTRAST WITH THE CUSTOMS of the Samaritans and their tradition of the prophet-like-Moses, John now presents us with the customs of the Jews, apparently based on the Mosaic tradition of an unexpected deliverance at the Passover. Now this practice of releasing a prisoner during the feast is otherwise unrecorded in historical accounts. For some commentators, it seems highly suspicious. Would a governor known for his inflexibility and brutality really have released a rabble-rousing insurrectionist who'd committed robbery and murder? Surely that would have drawn the ire of the authorities in Rome much more than the release of a serene and eccentric rabbi whose unearthly kingdom was, at least in any military sense, no threat to the might of the empire.

However, the human personality is complex—as we've seen with David. He was a great king and an outstanding warrior, capable of lavish kindness, deep contrition, profound sorrow and, contra wise, callous barbarism, serious hypocrisy and pitiless unforgiveness.

To suggest that Pilate is one-dimensionally merciless fails to come to grips with the paradoxes of human nature—especially since John has explicitly counterpointed David with Pilate through the parallel quote, 'It is not for us to execute anyone in Israel.'

Now, we have to hand it to Pilate. He really did try exceptionally hard to persuade the Jewish leaders to let Jesus go. He looked for loopholes and excuses in an attempt to get them to agree to the acquittal he wanted. But in the end, he was complicit with injustice and lawlessness. He is not exonerated just because of the pressure put on him. His was the decision that mattered. He knew he was condemning an innocent man. Under normal circumstances, he probably wouldn't have proposed releasing a criminal of the status of Barabbas. He'd raised the stakes to try and dissuade the chief priests and their followers from the course of action they were pursuing. He was no doubt surprised when they chose Barabbas. But, by that point, Pilate had tied himself up in a double bind. He'd taken a gamble and lost and, as a consequence, he'd also ceded authority to the crowd. Instead of being the one to make the decision, he'd allowed himself to be manoeuvred into a position where they were calling the shots.

Now some scholars suggest that John and Mark, who also mentions the custom of releasing a prisoner at the Passover, have invented this tradition to incriminate the Jews and exculpate the Romans. However, it simply seems likely that both writers were trying to explain the circumstances by which Roman jurisprudence, which emphasised four principles—equality under the law, presumption of innocence, the burden of proof on the accuser, and the disregard of unfair laws[120]—was sidestepped so that an innocent man was crucified.

---

120   See: roman-empire.net/roman-law/ (accessed 10 November 2024)

The Jews completely disregarded a multiplicity of their own Torah-based laws during Jesus' trial before Caiaphas,[121] but the Romans did very much the same when Jesus was arraigned before Pilate. John is not blame-shifting, he's pointing out the faults in both judicial arenas. The illegal operation of the court system and its blatant injustice was not restricted to one side.

---

121 See: thebiblesays.com/en/tough-topics/jesuss-trial-part-5-the-laws-of-practice-that-were-violated (accessed 10 November 2024)

'You worship what you do not know; we worship what we know, for salvation is from the Jews. But the hour is coming, and is now here, when the true worshippers will worship the Father in spirit and truth, for the Father is seeking such people to worship Him. God is spirit, and those who worship Him must worship in spirit and truth.'

The woman said to Him, 'I know that Messiah is coming (He who is called Christ). When He comes, He will tell us all things.'

Jesus said to her, 'I who speak to you am He.'

John 4:22–26 ESV

Part 5

They shouted back, 'No, not Him! Give us Barabbas!'
Now Barabbas had taken part in an uprising.

Then Pilate took Jesus and had him flogged. The soldiers twisted together a crown of thorns and put it on His head. They clothed Him in a purple robe and went up to Him again and again, saying, 'Hail, king of the Jews!'
And they slapped Him in the face.

John 18:40–19:3 NIV

5.1 Pilate's Downfall

'You worship what you do not know; we worship what we know, for salvation is from the Jews. But the hour is coming, and is now here, when the true worshippers will worship the Father in spirit and truth, for the Father is seeking such people to worship Him. God is spirit, and those who worship Him must worship in spirit and truth.'

The woman said to Him, 'I know that Messiah is coming (He who is called Christ). When He comes, He will tell us all things.'

Jesus said to her, 'I who speak to you am He.'

John 4:22–26[ESV]

They shouted back, 'No, not Him! Give us Barabbas!' Now Barabbas had taken part in an uprising.

Then Pilate took Jesus and had Him flogged.

The soldiers twisted together a crown of thorns and put it on His head. They clothed Him in a purple robe and went up to Him again and again, saying, 'Hail, king of the Jews!'

And they slapped Him in the face.

John 18:40–19:3[NIV]

REHOBOAM LOST HIS KINGSHIP AT SYCHAR. And Pilate lost his governorship there.

John repeatedly expected his readers to be aware of recent past history. As noted in *The Lustral Waters*, he introduced the name

Nicodemus, anticipating that his audience would know exactly who he meant—the famous Pharisee who had been nicknamed Naqdimon, 'Man of the Breakthrough', after his miraculous time-stopping prayer for God's intervention.

In these verses of the fourth chapter and their chiastic parallels at the end of the gospel, John once again anticipates being able to draw on his readers' awareness of contemporary affairs regarding what happened to Pilate in the years following the trial of Jesus. In these matched sections, there is on the one hand a discussion that, in context, is about:

- the sacred mountain of the Samaritans, the worship there, and the claim of Jesus to be the Messiah—the Restorer and Revealer of all things

    in counterpart to:

- the release of an insurrectionist who robbed and murdered during an uprising, plus the unjust condemnation of an innocent man

All these elements would come together once again in just a few short years to bring about the end of Pilate's governorship. The first century historian Flavius Josephus described what happened in *Jewish Antiquities*. A con-artist persuaded the Samaritans he knew where Moses had buried a cache of sacred vessels on Mount Gerizim. They gathered together at Tirathana, very near Sychar, intending to go up the mountain in a great multitude. However Pilate blocked their path with detachments of cavalry and infantry. Many pilgrims were killed, and many taken prisoner. Pilate executed the leaders along with many prominent citizens who had joined the gathering.

The Samaritan Senate was outraged at the massacre of so many innocents. Pilate had acted as if he were putting down an insurrection when, in their view, it was a legitimate religious gathering that had been convened with the hope of restoring true worship on their sacred mountain through retrieving holy vessels hidden by the prophet Moses. The Samaritan Senate sent an embassy to the Syrian governor, Lucius Vitellius, to protest Pilate's action. They accused Pilate of murder and insisted that the people who fled the soldiers were not in revolt but were simply seeking to save their lives. Vitellius, as Pilate's superior, ordered him to go to Rome to answer the accusations against him in a trial before the emperor. However, just before Pilate got there, Tiberius died. Pilate's subsequent movements became shrouded in legend.

John is using chiasmus to point out that Pilate reaped what he'd sowed. He might not have had to answer to higher Roman authority for the miscarriage of justice that featured in Jesus' trial, but he was nonetheless held culpable for a similar breach of the law just a short time later. He did not evade responsibility indefinitely.

Evidently, Pilate was adept at making a provocative hash of decisions that related to rebellion. He released the insurrectionist Barabbas under political pressure; he put down a non-existent insurrection of Samaritans; and when he first came to Judea, he almost caused an insurrection by deliberately allowing his legions to enter Jerusalem with effigies of the emperor on their standards.

Insurrection is the very reason Jesus went to Sychar. He was there to reunify the kingship of the Son of David under a single head. To do that He had to recapitulate the story of David's grandson Rehoboam so that, instead of a rebellion against the crown, there would be instead unparalleled devotion and loyalty expressed towards Himself as the messianic king.

In this process, He also revealed the heirs of David's mantle.

5.2 Barabbas

All of the gospels describe Barabbas, each adding slightly different detail. Matthew 27:16[CEV] labels Barabbas as a *'well-known terrorist'* and gives his full name in the next verse as Jesus Barabbas.[122] In Mark 15:7[NLT], it says he was a *'revolutionary who had committed murder in an uprising'*, while Luke 23:19[ESV] speaks of him as having *'been thrown into prison for an insurrection started in the city and for murder.'* John is very brief, describing him simply as a *'brigand'* or a *'bandit'*.

It appears that Pilate presented the leaders and their supporters with a choice between two men named Jesus. It was a common name—Greek for *Joshua*—and has echoes of the choice between two identical goats on the Day of Atonement—one for sacrifice and one to be driven away into the wilderness. Jesus had already imaged Himself as the goat to be cast out—the scapegoat—on the Day of Atonement the previous year when He took His disciples to the shrine of the goat-god Pan at Caesarea Philippi. It was there in front of the so-called Gates of Hell that Simon made his confession that Jesus was the Christ, the Messiah.

---

122 Not all manuscript copies say 'Jesus Barabbas', most just say 'Barabbas'.

Now, however, at the Passover, Jesus is also imaged as the goat to be sacrificed. Normally we think of a Passover *lamb* but, in God's original instructions for the feast,[123] the Hebrew word 'seh' can mean either a *young sheep* or a *young goat*—thus a *lamb* or a *kid*.

Furthermore, while Jesus' death occurred at the time of the Passover, it was also 'Little Yom Kippur', a traditional day of fasting for the firstborn in a family. This unusual day was set apart in memory of the last of the ten plagues and the death of the firstborn sons and animals of the Egyptians. It is unknown whether the Fast of the Firstborn, which commemorates gratitude for the salvation of the firstborn sons of Israel from the visit of the Angel of Death, was held in the first century. However possible references to it occur as early as the second century.[124] The fast has now been transferred to the day before, so as not to compete with the Passover itself.

Jesus would have been fasting throughout that day because He would have received no food as a prisoner. Moreover, we see here that He is recapitulating the storyline of the sons of Egypt, not that of the sons of Israel. It is not just the tragedies of the Jews that concern God. Jesus dies, as the firstborn of Egypt did, and He also rose and was saved from death, as the families of Israel were.

Not only is Jesus both the scapegoat of Yom Kippur and the perfect unblemished flockling of the Passover, He is also the substitute. Both Jesus and Barabbas are accused of some of the same crimes. Both are considered violent rabble-rousers,[125] inciters of treachery and insurrection against the state as well as spreaders of sedition. Barabbas was a notorious rebel who had been part of an uprising

---

123 Exodus 12:3-4
124 See: en.wikipedia.org/wiki/Fast_of_the_Firstborn (accessed 4 January 2025)
125 Recall: it's been only three days since Jesus plaited a whip and overturned the tables of the money-changers and traders in the Temple.

against Roman rule, while Jesus' claims to be the Messiah had challenged the Jewish authorities to take action to prevent an anticipated uprising. They accused Him of defying Caesar's rule by His claim to be king. The leaders basically put Pilate in a bind: if you don't agree that Jesus is a traitor to Rome, then you will be denounced by us as a traitor to Rome.

Andrew Wilson points out that the conviction of Jesus and the release of Barabbas is no mere exchange, but a substitution. 'Jesus doesn't just die *instead* of Barabbas; He dies in his place as his substitute, his representative... Few examples of substitutionary atonement in Scripture are clearer than Jesus, the innocent man, taking the penalty so that none remains for the guilty Barabbas.'[126] He adds, 'There is also an Exodus dimension here. The Gospels point out that freeing prisoners is a Passover custom. In other words, it happens in honour of the night when Pharaoh's firstborn son died so that God's firstborn son (Israel) could be released. But the Gospels raise a subtle question: Which of these two accused men is really God's firstborn son? The one whose name, Barabbas, means *son of the father*? Or the one claiming to be the Son of God? And is God's Son playing the part of Israel, escaping to freedom—or that of the Passover lamb, shedding his blood to liberate others?'

Now *son of the father*[127] is not the only possible meaning for Barabbas. It may also mean *son of the teacher*.[128] If this is accurate, it then suggests that Barabbas was the son of a leading Jewish rabbi. Yet it also evokes the great Teacher of Jewish tradition. The first verse of Ecclesiastes begins:

---

126 See:christianitytoday.com/2021/03/andrew-wilson-barabbas-story-prisoner-swap/ (accessed 16 November 2024)
127 From 'bar abba'.
128 From 'bar rabban'.

> 'These are the words of the Teacher, the son of David, king in Jerusalem.'
>
> Ecclesiastes 1:1^{BSB}

Solomon was the Teacher—or the Preacher. And therefore, the 'son of the Teacher' was Rehoboam who lacked the wisdom of his father—or, at least of his father in his earlier years—and who incited an insurrection against his own rule by promising higher taxes, greater abuse and a raised level of cruelty. With such a vote-winning combination of pledges, it's no surprise that spontaneous rebellion flared.

Both Rehoboam and Barabbas (who more truly represents Rehoboam's rival, Jeroboam) symbolise rash choices, adverse political might, and rebellious aggression. Jesus by contrast symbolises sacrificial choices, transcendent peace and covenantal defence.

When we look back at David, we see a stark contrast to Jesus as the Son of David. David reported to the assembly he summoned to Jerusalem that the Lord had not given him permission to build the Temple because:

> 'you are a man of war, and you have committed bloodshed.'
>
> 1 Chronicles 28:3^{ISV}

Many of us think of Uriah's murder in this regard but there is much more to the 'man of war and bloodshed' than simply that incident. Consider:

- the sacrifice of the sons of Saul and the violation of covenant with the House of Saul because of the request of the Gibeonites—an episode where he is directly compared to Pontius Pilate.
- the murder of Uriah and his squadron during the war for the city of Rabbah of Ammon

- the torture of the people of Rabbah of Ammon[129] once the citadel was taken
- the massacre of the Moabites by forcing them to lie on the ground and killing two of every three[130]
- his insistence on a census while refusing to listen to his commanders that this was not God-inspired. (Clearly, since a census was allowable in God's law providing an atonement fee was paid, David wasn't willing to pay the price. The people eventually paid a very high price when David was given three options for restitution and a plague angel came to visit the nation.)
- his perpetuation of the feud between Bethlehem of Judah and Gibeah of Benjamin instead of making the choice to heal it. This feud, in many ways, carried down the centuries even to Paul of Tarsus and Jesus—despite Esther of the tribe of Benjamin saving the Jews.
- his placing of Goliath's head outside Jerusalem, long before it belonged to the Israelites[131]
- his lies to the Philistine king, Achish, about where he was raiding—thus leaving the wives and children of his men and himself completely vulnerable and defenceless when he was called to join in the Philistine war against the Israelites.

---

129 See: versenotes.org/it-happened-in-the-spring/ (accessed 4 September 2024) In a curious twist, the wife of Solomon and the mother of his successor, Rehoboam, was from Ammon.

130 2 Samuel 8:2

131 See *The Lustral Waters* for the implications of David's action with respect to his taking of Jerusalem and making it his capital when it is outside of his own tribal territory. Also note the discussion there about the view of some scholars who regard Golgotha, *the place of the skull*, as the location where David planted the head.

Now, on that last point—just as David sought refuge with Achish against Saul's murderous pursuit, so Jeroboam sought refuge with Pharaoh against Solomon's murderous pursuit. Both of the hunted men had much the same reasons for seeking sanctuary in a foreign land. Just as it had been prophesied that the kingdom would be stripped from Saul and given to David, so it was prophesied that the kingdom would split and ten of twelve tribes would follow Jeroboam. In other words, the monarchy would pass from one ruling house to another. It would be given into the hands, not just of another family, but of another tribe entirely.

Jeroboam was a member of the tribe of Ephraim. He was descended from Joseph.

John's gospel does not use the expression 'Son of David', an expression of hope in the coming of the royal messiah. Instead he uses the phrase 'Son of Joseph', a term anticipating the coming of the war messiah.

The war that Jesus engages in is, however, one against the principalities and powers. It is not against flesh and blood. His weapons are love and truth, compassion and healing. He accepts the woman but He does not affirm her wrong thinking or ungodly behaviour.

In His recapitulation of the past, He does not affirm the wrong thinking or ungodly behaviour of Abraham or David, Rehoboam or Jeroboam, Ezra or Nehemiah, Caiaphas or Pilate either. He sets about righting their iniquities, and announces the need of the people for Living Water—the Holy Spirit—to cleanse the land of its long history of injustice and unrighteousness and to bring its people into wholeness.

5.3 Salvation is from the Jews

You worship what you do not know; we worship what we know, for salvation is from the Jews.

John 4:22^{ESV}

IN SAYING, 'YOU WORSHIP WHAT YOU DO NOT KNOW,' it would appear that Jesus is simply asserting that the Samaritans are ignorant. But is He saying that? And is it all of what He is saying?

In the Hebrew Scriptures, *'know'* is often used as a covenantal expression. Indeed *'know'* used in this way was not restricted to the Jews. When covenants between nations were broken, sometimes a king would lament to another, 'But I *know* you!'

Now, recall that Shechem was famously the seat of the Temple of Baal-Berith, *lord of the covenant*, and as well the site of multiple covenant affirmations—not to mention a few covenant violations. So is what Jesus really saying this: *'You Samaritans worship without understanding and where there is no true covenant'*? In other words, much as the Samaritan leaders would like to believe they are faithfully worshipping in accordance with the ancient ways, keeping the Torah in fidelity and truth, a covenant with the Most High God is missing—and, if you want it, I am here to rectify the problem.

For the Samaritans who adhered only to the Torah, the question of what mountain was the legitimate place to worship was a real obstacle.[132] Jerusalem is not mentioned in the Torah—the first five books of the Bible, the books of Moses—at all. Neither is Zion. Mount Moriah is mentioned but, as far as the Samaritans were concerned, it was misidentified. They believed Moreh, the place where Abraham had built the first altar to God in the land later promised to him for his descendants, was the same as Moriah. They thought that when Abraham was asked to sacrifice Isaac, he returned to the very first place he'd made an offering to God.

Now Jesus has not told the Samaritan woman that the Jews are right and her people are wrong when it comes to sacred mountains or their adherence to the Laws of Moses. What He has said is that it won't save you because salvation comes from the Jews.

Is this all that much different from Paul saying that the Law won't save you from sin? It's more subtle, that's certain. However it's still expressing the truth that it's not rules that make a difference, it's a Person. It's Jesus Himself, born of the Holy Spirit and a Jewish woman—through coming into covenant with Him. That's God's plan to usher us into salvation.

Jesus recognised the mental struggle of the woman and, before she could heap up a wall of denial about the Taheb being a Jew and run for her sanity, He confirmed her worst suspicions. He forced her to face the reality of who He is by bringing His identity out into the open.

Just as He forced Pontius Pilate. But with entirely different results.

---

132 Their temple on Mount Gerizim had been destroyed on the orders of John Hyrcanus, the Jewish ruler and high priest, in around 111 BC.

5.4 The Hour is Now

> *Woman, believe Me, the hour is coming when neither on this mountain nor in Jerusalem will you worship the Father...*
>
> *But the hour is coming, and is now here, when the true worshippers will worship the Father in spirit and truth.*
>
> John 4:21;23[ESV]

'THE HOUR IS COMING AND IS NOW HERE' is an expression repeatedly used by Jesus as John attests. He reports it here and also in the next chapter (John 5:25). In addition, a very similar saying is recounted in John 16:32. In both this chapter and chapter 16, Jesus mentions *'the hour is coming'* slightly in advance of the longer wording, and in chapter 5, He says it slightly afterwards.

The repetition highlights that the appointed time *really* has arrived. Back in the second chapter, Jesus remarked to His mother that His hour had not yet come. She'd just alerted Him to the lack of wine and He'd queried why she was involving Him. Yet despite it not being the appointed time, He summoned it to Himself, showing that He is Lord of Time in both its ordinary sense as well as all its appointed moments. It is not particularly extraordinary for water to be transformed into wine—it's a process that happens throughout the grape-growing season on vines throughout the world. But it is miraculous for that process to take minutes and not months.

Jesus created fine mature wine that was also *new* wine and, as noted in *The Summoning of Time*, the Hebrew word for *new wine* is derived from a word for *inheritance*. The provision of the wine for the wedding was symbolic of a return of a birthright and an overthrow of Anat, the dispossessor and the goddess who claimed to rule appointed time.

The meeting with the Samaritan woman links back to the wedding at Cana, not just through the references to appointed time, not just to a wildly extravagant return of inheritance, not just to echoes of ancient encounters at wells with their own religious connotations of time,[133] but with that very explicit form of address, 'Woman.'[134]

In Aramaic, *woman* was 'anath'—the same as the Greek form of the Canaanite name, Anat. We tend to overlook the possibility that, because educated Jews of the first century knew more than one language, their choice of wording might actually be influenced by the possibility of cross-cultural allusion.

Jesus was engaged in a war with the hierarchy of the Canaanite pantheon—this is the second battle that John has outlined where Anat is a major target. Another battle ensues in the garden outside the tomb after the resurrection during His encounter with Mary

---

133 Recall Plutarch's analysis of Egyptian religion and his comment, 'Time is the wife of water.' Perhaps it was a reference to time as measured by the monthly progression of lunar phases and the tides that vary according to those phases.

134 For a detailed look at the issues surrounding the use of 'Woman' as a form of address particularly in reference to Mary, the mother of Jesus, see *The Summoning of Time*. Sometimes the word is used to evoke Eve and sometimes it's used to evoke Anat. Also note: *woman* is used 23 times in the gospel of John. 17 of these times it is used simply to identify the person and 6 times it is used as a mode of address, on 5 different occasions, for 4 different women—Mary, the mother of Jesus, at Cana and the Cross; Mary Magdalene at the resurrection; the woman at the well in Samaria and the woman caught in adultery.

Magdalene.¹³⁵ In each case, Jesus interacts with a woman—two named Mary—as He campaigns against Anat. Indeed, I wonder if the third is yet another Mary and not Photini, as is traditional. Or if, as James McGrath has suggested, Photini is the Greek form of an Aramaic or Hebrew name.

Now in the previous chapter, the dialogue between Jesus and Nicodemus encodes multiple puns on this renowned Pharisee's real name: Buni ben Gurion. Nicodemus is the nickname he received as the result of a miraculous answer to prayer that spread his fame throughout the Jewish world. I think a similar thing is happening here: the woman's nickname is Photini and her real name is coded into the conversation between Jesus and herself.

My suggestion is that she was called by some variation on Neharah, Nahar or Nora.¹³⁶ The word 'neharah' or 'na'arah', *young woman* or *maiden*, is derived from 'nahar', *light, shining, radiance, flowing* or *stream*. It can also refer to a *gathering of people*—precisely what she achieves.¹³⁷ Although *young* and *maiden* are unlikely descriptors

---

135   See *The Summoning of Time*, the second book in this series.
136   The modern name Nora may trace its origin back to this ancient word. There are several different possible roots for modern Nora, depending on its ethnic origin. One possibility is that it is a diminutive of Honora, *honour*; a second possible root is Eleanor, of unknown origin but possibly originating in Helen, usually said to mean *light*—but more likely meaning *icon* or *mediator of divine light*. The third possibility is actually related back to 'nahar'. It is the modern Arabic name, Nora, also spelled Nura, from Arabic, 'nur', *light*.
137   If it is correct that her name is some variation on Nahar, then her conversation with Jesus actually involves a name covenant—very similar to the name covenant between Himself and Simon in which there is an exchange of names: Simon calls Jesus 'Messiah', Jesus then calls him 'Peter' or 'Cephas'. Here too in this encounter with the Samaritan woman there is the naming of Jesus as the Messiah or the Christ. Name covenants precede threshold covenants and these threshold covenants are enacted across the next few days as Jesus accepts Samaritan hospitality. See: Anne Hamilton, *Name Covenant—Invitation to Friendship: Strategies for the Threshold #3*, Armour Books 2018

of her, there is precedent for the use of the word 'na'arah' to describe a widow: this is the term Boaz uses when he first sees Ruth in his fields, not realising either her foreign background or her in-law relationship to him. Moreover the various senses of 'nahar'—*flowing, stream* and *gathering of people*—are covered in the Samaritan woman's dialogue with Jesus, or in its immediate aftermath,[138] while her traditional name Photini is alluded to in the *light, shining* and *radiance* aspects of 'nahar'.

Further, 'nahar' reminds us of the Nahor clan of Aram-Naharaim, the land where eleven of the twelve patriarchs of Israel were born. Nahor was the brother of both Abram and Sarai as well as the grandfather of Laban. The clan of Nahor were the relatives that Jacob, apparently, did not tell of his allegiance to God Most High—so, if this name for the Samaritan woman is correct—we see yet a further healing of history in her meeting with Jesus. The spiritually disenfranchised kin of Abraham and his grandson Jacob—the forefather of all the tribes of Israel—were given an opportunity by Jesus to know the Word made flesh. This multi-level healing echoes the ancient encounters at the well in Aram-Naharaim where, in one generation, Abraham's servant met Rebekah and, in the next generation, her son Jacob met Rachel—yet, it also recapitulates the stories since it yields a different outcome.

---

138 The most obvious Greek rendering of Nahar or Na'ar is not, in fact, Photini. Rather it would be Nereus, the name of a sea-god in Greek mythology. But maybe it was a little too close to Nero for comfort; hence the choice of Photini. The water-deity Nereus was the son of Pontus and Gaia, making an exceptional link back to the dominant name in the chiastic section: Pontius Pilate. Another Hebrew word for *stream*, also with a sense of *living, flowing water* is 'nachal' or 'nakal'. This is the word repeatedly used by Deborah in her song (Judges 5:2–31) to describe the river that flash-flooded and swept away the forces of Sisera, the Canaanite general who worshipped the war-goddesses Anat and Astarte. (See *The Summoning of Time*.)

Now the battles between Jesus and Anat are not wild melees where bystanders fall as collateral damage—they are superficially unremarkable events that display no sign whatsoever of the fierce combat that is actually going on. In the simplest of ways, Jesus topples all of Anat's various claims to judge, to choose the divine king, to be a cupbearer to that divine king, to dispossess, and to govern appointed time.

There's no question in my mind that the Samaritan woman had no idea she'd stepped into a warzone that day. Neither did any of the disciples have a clue what was really transpiring. I believe it would have taken years for John to connect the dots and realise that, at the appointed hour—around the sixth—both Pontius Pilate and a Samaritan woman took action, each in their own way, to announce the kingship of Jesus.

5.5 In Spirit and Truth

God is spirit, and those who worship Him must worship in spirit and truth.

John 4:24^{ESV}

JOHN SHOWS US A SAVIOUR willing to cross every national, racial and social barrier to appoint His kingmaker, cupbearer and first evangelist. It isn't *just* about saving a soul so that the only alteration in her life is that she worships in Spirit and truth, wherever she is, and no longer needs to concern herself with mountains of any kind.

Jesus, having basically said 'any place' is suitable for the worship of God in Spirit and truth, undercut the claim of the Samaritans for Mount Gerizim and the Jewish counterclaim for Mount Zion. He implicitly exposed the desire for prestige and eminence in both cases.

To keep covenant with God, it's not a matter of the right place but the right Person. So, the people now have to remain loyal to Jesus as the Tehab, not return to Moses as their primary law-giver.[139]

Within a few years, their allegiance was seriously tested when along came a charlatan who claimed he knew where Moses had hidden some sacred vessels on Mount Gerizim. It wasn't just that he appealed to the Samaritan sense of right worship, he also drew on their desire to put the Jews in their place by showing that they'd got something older and holier than Herod's temple which had neither Ark nor Tabernacle.

Now it's not particularly difficult to detect the spirit behind that test as Anat, the orchestrator of massacres. After all, until Jesus came along, she'd held the territory of Shechem in her blood-stained grip—going back at least until the time of the massacre of its citizens by Levi and Simeon and also including the era when Abimelech, son of Gideon, used money from the temple of Baal-Berith to finance the massacre of his brothers. Anat, of course, wants to regain her losses after Jesus is acclaimed the Messiah, the Taheb. She sees herself as the one who dispossesses, not the

---

[139] The conflict between loyalty to Jesus and to a particular mountain was clearly recognised by Julian the Apostate, the nephew of Constantine the Great. Julian had been brought up in the Christian faith but had converted to Pythagorean theurgy and, when he assumed one of the thrones of a suddenly divided empire (much like Jeroboam in an earlier age), he wanted to reintroduce paganism. But he believed that it wouldn't be simple and that Christianity hadn't been so much imposed on the empire by his uncle but was, in fact, the people's choice. He therefore wanted to set up an ethical alternative that would be attractive to the people, and he promoted Pythagoreanism. But he also tried to rebuild the Temple in Jerusalem in 363 AD and reinstate animal sacrifice. Part of his motivation was to falsify the prophecy of Jesus about the Temple. The pagan historian Ammianus Marcellinus records earthquakes, landslides, and balls of fire coming out of the ground that all prevented the restoration. Many Christians also recorded their testimony about the destructive impact of these events. Warren H Carroll, *A History of Christendom, Vol. 1, The Founding of Christendom*, Christendom Press 2004

one dispossessed. She sees herself as the judge amongst the divine beings, the one who dispenses inheritance and the one with the right to confer kingship. She'd have been enraged that, from her perspective, a nondescript nameless woman had usurped her role as kingmaker and cupbearer amongst the gods. The elder-gods assisting her were the local divinities: Nergal, the Mesopotamian patron of war, disease and death, and his Canaanite counterpart, Resheph, patron of war, plague and death.

Together they try to bring about an end to the reconciliation and restoration that Jesus had forged in the people and in the land. It's unclear when Philip went to Samaria—before or after Pilate's massacre—but the people were open to his preaching and when Peter and John arrived, they were open to the Holy Spirit, to the Living Water that Jesus had promised.

John had reported that Nicodemus had learned the new birth would come in Spirit and water. Now John reveals that Jesus offered the woman Spirit and Truth. Slowly he is building our understanding of the nature of the Living Water. It is the flow of Truth and accompanies our new birth as we become the Bride of Christ, the Temple of the Holy Spirit, the Tabernacle of His in-dwelling, a living stone within His city and a part of His body.

5.6 I AM

The woman said to Him, 'I know that Messiah is coming (He who is called Christ). When He comes, He will tell us all things.'
Jesus said to her, 'I who speak to you am He.'

John 4:25–26^{ESV}

Then Pilate took Jesus and had Him flogged. The soldiers twisted together a crown of thorns and put it on His head. They clothed Him in a purple robe and went up to Him again and again, saying, 'Hail, king of the Jews!' And they slapped Him in the face.

John 19:1–3^{NIV}

JOHN HASN'T GIVEN US ALL THE DETAILS of Jesus' trial. Just as he's left out any account of the fame of Nicodemus or the fate of Pilate, apparently expecting his readers to fill in the gaps themselves from common knowledge, so too here he's omitted some finer elements. Pilate has washed his hands of the situation, quite literally, but John doesn't mention that.[140] Nor does he refer to the dream of Pilate's wife or her message to her husband to have nothing to do with Jesus.[141] Neither does he mention about a

---

140 'When Pilate saw that he was getting nowhere, but that instead an uproar was starting, he took water and washed his hands in front of the crowd. "I am innocent of this man's blood," he said. "It is your responsibility!"' (Matthew 27:24^{NIV})

141 'While Pilate was sitting on the judge's seat, his wife sent him this message: "Don't have anything to do with that innocent man, for I have suffered a great deal today in a dream because of him."' (Matthew 27:19^{NIV})

detail significant to the chiasmus in this scene where the soldiers are having some vicious fun. Once again, it seems, John is relying on his readers' awareness of the contents of other gospel records:

> *They blindfolded Him and asked, 'Prophesy, who is it that struck You?'*
>
> Luke 22:64[AMP]

The woman describes the Messiah in terms of the Taheb: the prophet-like-Moses who will tell us all things. Along with the brutal flogging and mocking coronation that follow at Pilate's order are the jibes of the soldiers to prophesy—to know the unknowable, even blindfolded.

If the woman actually used either the term 'Messiah' or 'Christ' (and John is not simply translating 'Taheb' into a more recognisable word), then she referred to Jesus as *the anointed one*. Both prophets and kings were anointed—and so the designation works whatever she meant. The Jews were looking for a king, the Samaritans for a prophet.

The soldiers crowned the king, jeering and taunting, with a crown of thorns. It was rare in ancient days for kings to wear full-circlet crowns; it was far more common for a half-circle diadem to be worn.[142] It was even quite rare for full-surround crowns to be part of the apparel of the godlings and goddesses—one of the exceptions being, naturally, Anat. The crown of thorns is more reminiscent of the wreath worn by a bridegroom, and it's at this point in the narrative—reading forward instead of chiastically—that the bridal imagery begins to build. The symbolism culminates in the

---

142   See, for example regarding a full circular crown, the crown of the king of the Ammonites:

digitalcommons.andrews.edu/cgi/viewcontent.cgi?referer=&httpsredir= 1&article=1228&context=auss (accessed 20 July 2024)

cry of Bridegroom at the Cross, 'It is finished! It is consummated!' and the extravagant supply of myrrh, the traditional oil of joy for a wedding, by the Friend of the Bridegroom.

Isaiah prophesied of this moment:

> *He was pierced for our transgressions, He was crushed for our iniquities; the punishment that brought us peace was upon Him, and by His stripes we are healed.*
>
> Isaiah 53:5[BSB]

So had the psalmist who penned the tenth of the Songs of Ascent:

> *My back is covered with cuts, as if a farmer had ploughed long furrows.*[143]
>
> Psalm 129:3[NLT]

For the woman of Samaria, the Restorer has come: the one who heals, the one who binds up the wounds of the past. She has recognised Truth but awaits confirmation from Him. In contrast, the Jewish leaders and the Roman auxiliaries, including Pilate, have denied the Truth, and deliberately ignored Him or laughed at Him. So Jesus is silent for them—they've closed their minds and hearts.

But both the mind and heart of the woman of Samaria are open. So Jesus reveals to her that He is not only greater than Jacob who built the well, not only greater than Moses, in fact He's far greater than the Taheb, the promised prophet-like-Moses. He is I AM, the One who spoke to Moses from the burning bush.

The Greek is clearer than most English translations. It's not so much, *'I who speak to you am He,'* as *'I AM is speaking to you.'*

---

[143] The Canaanite word for *furrow* is almost identical to the name of the war goddess 'Anat'.

Jesus discloses to the woman that He is God incarnate.

And, probably fortunately for her as she tried to process this stunning announcement, the disciples returned right at that moment.

These two chiastic scenes are a challenge today to those of us who call ourselves 'believers'. We might declare 'Jesus is Lord', but what does our surrender to Him look like? Too many times our behaviour is such a mockery of the holy that we are like those soldiers hailing Jesus as king but slapping Him in the face with our pride, unforgiveness, selfishness and hypocrisy.

Perhaps we aren't broken enough, as the woman of Samaria was, to allow Truth to speak and for the Living Water to flow into our lives.

PART SIX

Just then His disciples came back. They marvelled that He was talking with a woman, but no one said, 'What do You seek?' or, 'Why are You talking with her?'

So the woman left her water jar and went away into town and said to the people, 'Come, see a man who told me all that I ever did. Can this be the Christ?' They went out of the town and were coming to Him.

Meanwhile the disciples were urging Him, saying, 'Rabbi, eat.'

But He said to them, 'I have food to eat that you do not know about.'

So the disciples said to one another, 'Has anyone brought Him something to eat?'

Jesus said to them, 'My food is to do the will of Him who sent Me and to accomplish His work. Do you not say, "There are yet four months, then comes the harvest"? Look, I tell you, lift up your eyes, and see that the fields are white for harvest. Already the one who reaps is receiving wages and gathering fruit for eternal life, so that sower and reaper may rejoice together. For here the saying holds true, "One sows and another reaps." I sent you to reap that for which you did not labour. Others have laboured, and you have entered into their labour.'

Many Samaritans from that town believed in Him because of the woman's testimony, 'He told me all that I ever did.' So when the Samaritans came to Him, they asked Him to stay with them, and He stayed there two days. And many more believed because of His word.

They said to the woman, 'It is no longer because of what you said that we believe, for we have heard for ourselves, and we know that this is indeed the Saviour of the world.'

John 4:27-42   ESV

John 19:4-7 NIV

Once more Pilate came out and said to the Jews gathered there, 'Look, I am bringing Him out to you to let you know that I find no basis for a charge against Him.' When Jesus came out wearing the crown of thorns and the purple robe, Pilate said to them, 'Here is the man!'

As soon as the chief priests and their officials saw Him, they shouted, 'Crucify! Crucify!'

But Pilate answered, 'You take Him and crucify Him. As for me, I find no basis for a charge against Him.'

The Jewish leaders insisted, 'We have a law, and according to that law He must die, because He claimed to be the Son of God.'

6.1 SEE A MAN

Just then His disciples came back. They marvelled that He was talking with a woman, but no one said, 'What do You seek?' or, 'Why are You talking with her?'

So the woman left her water jar and went away into town and said to the people, 'Come, see a man who told me all that I ever did. Can this be the Christ?' They went out of the town and were coming to Him.

John 4:27–30^{ESV}

Once more Pilate came out and said to the Jews gathered there, 'Look, I am bringing Him out to you to let you know that I find no basis for a charge against Him.' When Jesus came out wearing the crown of thorns and the purple robe, Pilate said to them, 'Here is the man!'

John 19:4–5^{NIV}

'COME, SEE A MAN…' says the woman.

'Here is the man!' says Pilate.

We might even be reminded of Nathan's words when David expressed outrage that a rich man should steal a poor man's lamb to prepare a feast for a visitor: *'You are the man!'*[144] After all, David and Pilate have been compared previously. Here once again, there are parallels as both rulers condemn an innocent man for personal political gain—David orders the murder of Uriah and Pilate orders the execution of Jesus.

Belief and unbelief are contrasted in these two scenes that feature a gathering. The two major players in each scene are now joined by others: the disciples in the first instance, the Jewish leaders in the second. The disciples are silent at the well, Jesus is silent facing His detractors.

Judgment is also contrasted in these episodes. The woman has indicated, by her actions that, regardless of the reception she receives back in town, she's returning. She has enough faith to take the extraordinary step of leaving her water jar behind. This is a vessel that has more than the usual high value for such an important domestic article—it's been used to transport sacred well water. It may have been considered *holy, consecrated, set apart*.

Even when ordinary jars used at ordinary wells broke, the pieces were often kept—the bigger ones as dishes, the smaller pieces as potsherds for scraping diseased skin. The contact between the shard and a flow of water was understood to have invested it with purifying power.[145]

---

144 2 Samuel 12:7 — here Nathan has told a parable to show to David the enormity of his actions and to lure him into judging himself. David was a very rich man (his marriage to Abigail probably made him the wealthiest man in the entire country even before he became king—likely richer than Saul ever was) and he has at least seven wives at this point, not counting concubines. To take Uriah's wife, the 'ewe lamb' of Nathan's parable, was unconscionable.

145 John Loren Sandford and Paula Sandford, *The Elijah Task: A Call to Today's Prophets and Intercessors*, Spring Arbor Distributors, 1980

Pilate has, at this point, according to Matthew's account,[146] already washed his hands, disclaiming any responsibility for the decision. But that action had no power—and, as we have seen, he reaped as he sowed.

Just as sin entered the world through a choice, now salvation enters through a choice.

---

146 Matthew 27:24

6.2 The Barriers Fall

Just then His disciples came back. They marvelled that He was talking with a woman, but no one said, 'What do You seek?' or, 'Why are You talking with her?'

John 4:27ESV

THE USUAL RABBINIC ATTITUDE TOWARDS WOMEN was hostile and was encoded in the following precepts:[147]

- 'Let no one talk with a woman in the street, no, not with his own wife.'
- 'Better that the words of the law should be burnt than delivered to a woman.'
- 'Each time that a man prolongs converse with a woman he causes evil to himself, and desists from the law, and in the end inherits Gehenna.'[148]

It wasn't just that men didn't talk to women. Women didn't talk to men, either. Unless, according to John Sandford, they belonged

---

147   William Barclay, *The Gospel of John Volume 1, The Daily Study Bible*, The Saint Andrew Press, Edinburgh, 1963
148   Gehenna was the place of hellfire.

to one of two exceptional groups—either harlots or prophets. He considers the evidence to be sufficient to consider she was a prophet.[149]

The disciples *'marvelled'*. They were obviously stunned. Either they were speechless with shock or else they took refuge in silence because they simply didn't know how to process what they'd just witnessed firsthand. It was too revolutionary, too counter-cultural, too radical. Perhaps they might have suspected something beforehand but now they were sure: the attitude of Jesus was diametrically opposed to that of other rabbinic teachers. He was not only willing to talk to a woman, but to teach her as well, unafraid of the traditional prohibitions and the curse of hellfire that was said to await Him.

The respect of the disciples for Jesus had clearly reached the stage where they weren't about to raise an immediate protest or even mildly question Him: they had learned to wait patiently for answers. Jesus would have His reasons. Whatever His purpose in taking down the double barrier between men and women as well as between Jews and Samaritans, the disciples had come to trust Him enough to keep their mouths shut and wait until the time was right to discover His motives.

Jesus was opening up the whole question of women studying and learning in an iconoclastic, ground-breaking way. At this point in Jesus' ministry, there were obviously no women travelling with the disciples or they wouldn't have been so astounded. But things were about to change. It would not be long before women would be sitting at the feet of Jesus and drinking of the Living Water, just as the men did.

---

149 John Loren Sandford and Paula Sandford, *The Elijah Task: A Call to Today's Prophets and Intercessors*, Spring Arbor Distributors, 1980

Soon afterward, Jesus began going around from one city and village to another, preaching and proclaiming the good news of the kingdom of God. The twelve [disciples] were with Him, and also some women who had been healed of evil spirits and diseases: Mary, called Magdalene... from whom seven demons had come out, and Joanna, the wife of Chuza, Herod's household steward, and Susanna, and many others who were contributing to their support out of their private means [as was the custom for a rabbi's disciples].

Luke 8:1–3^{AMP}

6.3 THE KING HAS COME

'Can this be the Christ?'
They went out of the town and were coming to Him.

John 4:30^{ESV}

ON THE ONE HAND, THE SAMARITANS eagerly check out the woman's invitation to see for themselves whether the Taheb had come. On the other, Jesus was paraded before the Jewish leaders with a crown and purple robe—the apparel of a king or a high priest.

Pilate has done his examination. In the chiastic passage, the people of Samaria are about to do theirs. They would not have been completely clueless. A motley band of twelve strangers would have been watched—very closely. In case they were troublemakers, possibly even bandits or revolutionaries on the run. So the Samaritans would have scrutinised the disciples as they bought food. They'd have listened carefully to any casual conversation and noted their Galilean, not Judean, origin. They'd have already reached the conclusion their teacher was a very unusual one—since His personal following was largely tradesmen, not scholars. The most educated amongst them was probably the reformed tax collector. The Samaritans may not have picked up on all of this during their interaction with Jesus' disciples, but they'd have formed an overall picture. They'd have realised there was a rabbi out by their sacred well and He was… very, very *different*.

So when the woman came back, the tiny spark of curiosity that the disciples had ignited would have been fanned into flame by her words. If she was wrong, she was wrong. No doubt many well-meaning people had had their hopes raised over the centuries and been wrong. But if she was right, then to let the stranger pass through and not discern the truth of His identity would have been a dereliction of the faith passed onto them by their ancestors.

In this, we see the massive contrast between the Samaritans and the Jewish leaders: the chief priests had abandoned the faith passed down to them. Rather than acknowledge the king, they conspired to kill Him.

6.4 The Harvest

Meanwhile the disciples were urging Him, saying, 'Rabbi, eat.'

But He said to them, 'I have food to eat that you do not know about.'

So the disciples said to one another, 'Has anyone brought Him something to eat?'

Jesus said to them, 'My food is to do the will of Him who sent Me and to accomplish His work. Do you not say, "There are yet four months, then comes the harvest"? Look, I tell you, lift up your eyes, and see that the fields are white for harvest. Already the one who reaps is receiving wages and gathering fruit for eternal life, so that sower and reaper may rejoice together. For here the saying holds true, "One sows and another reaps." I sent you to reap that for which you did not labour. Others have laboured, and you have entered into their labour.'

John 4:31–38^{ESV}

WITH THE WOMAN JESUS HAD TALKED about water; now with the disciples He talks about food.[150]

John here is foreshadowing the great miracle of the loaves and fishes, just two chapters away. There it is physical food Jesus provides, here it is spiritual food. *'My food,'* He says, *'is to do the will of Him who sent Me and to accomplish His work.'* In this context, *'will'* does not just mean the *desires* and *purposes* of God, it refers to the *destiny* that has been laid out for Jesus in being sent to earth.

Jesus is the *sent one*. He describes His task as *'to do the will of Him who sent Me'* and then He remarks that He *sent* the disciples to reap that for which they did not labour. There are two different words for *sent* in those verses. The first is 'pempein' and it appears 27 times in John's gospel. The second is 'apostellein', from which we get the word 'apostle', *the sent one*, and it appears 17 times. Altogether these words for *sent* occur 44 times.[151]

17 connects back to the statement of Jesus to the woman: 'I AM'. The very oldest and most archaic form of the Hebrew name of God, 'I AM', has a gematria of 17.[152]

---

150   The disciples have gone to seek food amongst foreigners as once Joseph's brothers sought food amongst the foreigners of Egypt. Not only is their search in vicinity of Joseph's tomb, a reminder of the story of Joseph and his brothers, but they are also out seeking in the very same place Joseph was looking for his brothers when he met a stranger who asked him, 'Who are you looking for?' That stranger foreshadows Jesus at the resurrection asking Mary the Magdalene, 'Who are you looking for?' (See: *The Summoning of Time*). The disciples as they scout for food happen to be wandering around, just as Joseph was, in the last place he was to know freedom before being sold into captivity by his brothers.

151   See the third book in this series, *The Lustral Waters*, for an extensive discussion of multiples of 11 and 22 in John's gospel.

This numerical patterning with its encoding of 'I Am' and its signal of *sending* reinforces the identity of Jesus as the Taheb, the prophet-like-Moses, because it harks back to the revelation at the burning bush and the sending by 'I Am':

> *God said to Moses, 'I Am who I Am. This is what you are to say to the Israelites: "I Am has sent me to you."'*
>
> Exodus 3:14^{BSB}

Just as 'I Am' sent Moses out to liberate His people, now Jesus is sending His disciples out to liberate the people and to heal the land. But someone has been there before them. Jesus doesn't say who. But someone else has ploughed the ground and someone else has broadcast the seeds of the word and someone else has watered them and someone else has weeded around them and someone else has fertilised the ground—and God has given the increase. The disciples have arrived just in time to share in the joy and the bounty of the harvest that has reached full ripening.

And once again we have a reference to an anomaly of time. In John's second chapter, we learn of wine that was produced from water in an astonishingly compressed time span for a wedding at Cana.[153] In chapter three, we are introduced to Nicodemus—a man famous in the gospel for a discussion about being born again, but who was famous outside the gospel as the miracle-working 'Man of the Breakthrough' for whom time reversed. Now we have Jesus mentioning what was apparently a proverb, *'There are yet*

---

152 See the first book in this series, *The Elijah Tapestry*, for an extensive discussion of the use of 17 throughout early Christian writing. It is not the value of Yahweh, which does NOT mean 'I Am who I Am' but rather means 'He is who He is'. The word for 'I Am who I Am' given in Exodus 3:14 is Ehyeh. The most primitive form of this is 'aahweh'. Yahweh has a numerical value of 26, Ehyeh has a numerical value of 21 and 'aahweh' has a numerical value of 17.

153 See *The Summoning of Time*, the second book in this series.

four months, then comes the harvest,' basically saying that you can't plant a seed and expect it to grow straight away.[154] It takes months for the seed to sprout, the blade to rise through the dark earth, the head to form and then come to maturity.

Normally.

But here in Sychar, the timing is on a different clock. Jesus is telling the disciples that they are about to witness the fulfilment of the prophecy of Amos:

> *The days are going to come, declares the Lord, when the one who ploughs will catch up to the one who harvests, and the one who stomps on grapes will catch up to the one who plants. New wine will drip from the mountains and flow from all the hills.*
>
> Amos 9:13[GWT]

Several of the disciples have already been present for the production of *new wine* according to a divine timetable.[155] At

---

154 It would be difficult for it to be meant literally if it applied to a wheat harvest which was celebrated at Pentecost. Four months before Pentecost is a month after Hanukkah and a month before Purim. There would have been no festival in Jerusalem, as is described Jesus was attending just prior to this interlude in John 4:45. If it were the barley harvest that Jesus was referring to, a four month timespan would mean He was speaking about ten days before the Feast of Hanukkah, the *Festival of Lights* or *Feast of Dedication*. It's therefore winter and unlikely any sign of a crop would be evident. Furthermore, if it's winter, any assumptions about the woman's immorality based on the time of day she's at the well fly right out the window. She'd actually want to come during warmer hours, not in the chill of the early morning. The temperature variation at that time of year in the vicinity of Shechem is 5°C (41°F) minimum to 17°C (63°F) maximum.

155 On the topic of a divine timetable, how long did Jesus take to make the wine at Cana? Assuming that the relativistic time factor, 1 day = 1000 years, was in operation, it would have been about 36 minutes. Not including any ageing for *fine* wine.

Cana they witnessed the transformation of water to wine and, since 'new wine' is symbolic of *inheritance*, they would already be aware that the coming age is less about actual wine than about a return of birthright.

William Barclay points out: 'It was the dream of the golden age that sowing and reaping, planting and harvesting, would follow hard upon the heels of each other. There would be such fertility that the old days of waiting will be at an end.'[156] This is the promise of God given in the days of Moses as a blessing for obedience:

> *Your threshing season will overlap with the grape harvest, and your grape harvest will overlap with the season of planting grain. You will eat your fill and live securely in your own land.*
>
> Leviticus 26:5[NLT]

So, with the knowledge that the cryptic statements of Jesus point to greater spiritual realities, what did the disciples make of His words about the harvest? Did they decide He was talking about the sprouting fields of wheat they could see around them? That was, at best, a mere shadow of those greater realities Jesus wanted to open their eyes to. I think they were perhaps meant to understand at least three things:

- First, in the seasons promised by the Lord, there is no winter.

- Second, we often reap the benefit of someone else's labour. And that means that there will be times when our own labour yields little or even no result. But we are not to be discouraged because of that. Because it is the Lord who gives the increase, and He gives it at the right time.

---

156 William Barclay, *The Gospel of John Volume 1, The Daily Study Bible*, The Saint Andrew Press, Edinburgh, 1963

- Third, Jesus is declaring the coming of that golden age—the era of the Messiah—when the seed is planted and immediately the harvest is ready. That is, the word is spoken and, straight away, the fulfilment comes. This third aspect is one of the themes of the story that follows right after that of the Samaritan ingathering—that of the healing of the royal official's son.

6.5 Thorns and Harvest

Look, I tell you, lift up your eyes, and see that the fields are white for harvest.

Already the one who reaps is receiving wages and gathering fruit for eternal life, so that sower and reaper may rejoice together.

John 4:35–36[NIV]

When Jesus came out wearing the crown of thorns and the purple robe, Pilate said to them, 'Here is the man!'

As soon as the chief priests and their officials saw Him, they shouted, 'Crucify! Crucify!'

But Pilate answered, 'You take Him and crucify Him. As for me, I find no basis for a charge against Him.'

John 19:5–6[NIV]

IN HEBREW, THE WORDS FOR *harvest* and *thorn* are related via head-rhyme. *Thorn*, first mentioned by God as the curse that will befall the land because of the choice of Adam and Eve, is 'qots'. *Harvest* is 'qatsiyr', with additional connotations of *severed, cut off, reaped, fruit, lopped off, limb* and *time*. Perhaps the relationship between the two words revolves around the thought that thorns need to be cut off, just as a harvest needs to be cut down. Or perhaps it's that, since the fall, there will be thorns and thistles mixed in with every harvest.

Thorns have featured prominently in the history of God's dealing with Israel, quite apart from the decree in Eden that the ground will yield thorns and thistles even while the farmer was hoping for a good harvest. The bush that Moses saw burning but not being consumed was a thornbush on a mountain whose name means *thorny*: Mount Sinai. The mountain of law-giving was *thorny*, just as the mountain of temple sacrifice was *dry*. Yet the place of the Temple was also Mount Moriah,[157] where once a ram was caught in a thorn thicket as a substitute offering for the life of Isaac.

Now the Temple was built on a threshing floor of the Jebusites, the Canaanite people who had built the fortress of Zion. This indicates that the site of the Temple was originally associated with a harvest. In addition, perhaps that earlier mention of the ram in the thicket indicates Mount Moriah had *always* been a threshing floor, even in the time of Abraham. After all, threshing floors were deliberately surrounded by thorn hedges in order to keep out wild animals that might eat the sheaves of grain at harvest time, while they were piled up in heaps and the farmers were waiting for the right wind that would enable it to be winnowed. Thus the ram had been caught in the thicket while trying to get through it to the grain.

At the moment the chief priests were shouting 'Crucify!' they were probably standing on one of the porticoes joining the Antonia Fortress to the Temple—they were therefore on, or very near, that ancient threshing floor. Perhaps in the constant circling of Pilate, back and forward, in and out of the Fortress, repeatedly taking Jesus with him to question, we are meant to see a movement very similar to a threshing.

---

157 The Samaritans would have disputed this. They considered Moriah to be Moreh, the place where Abram had built that first altar to God in the land promised to his descendants.

It was Passover—the time of the barley harvest. It was two days until the Feast of Firstfruits when the Israelites would be required to bring a sheaf of the first grain that had been harvested. Although this would make the threshing out of sequence, that is the whole point of the time anomalies that have been prominent to this point in the gospel, but are also mentioned in respect to the harvest itself.

The first threshing floor mentioned in Scripture is Goren ha'Atad, *threshing floor of the thornbush*, where the Egyptians camped for seven days on the far side of the Jordan while bringing Jacob's body back to the land of his forefathers. It was there at Goren ha'Atad that Joseph spent a week in mourning for Jacob. The place and time of his lamentation begs the question: was he was trying to communicate with his deceased father? Threshing floors were considered to be 'thin places' where the borderlands between heaven and earth were slender, and divination was therefore easier.[158] When someone wanted to consult the gods, they could go to a shrine in an alcove on a threshing floor, perhaps even sleep there hoping for a revelatory dream. A threshing floor was considered ideal for the witnessing of agreements by various deities. Marriages were solemnised there, war councils held, and judgments delivered.

The word 'atad' may not just be *thornbush* or *bramble*, but perhaps derive from Hebrew 'at' and thus have the sense of *necromancy—divination by consulting the dead*.

---

158   When Joseph sends his steward after his brothers to collect the silver cup that has been secreted in Benjamin's sack, the steward exclaims: *'Isn't this the cup my master drinks from and also uses for divination? This is a wicked thing you have done.'* (Genesis 44:5[NIV]) It's difficult to tell, given that the whole scene is one of deceit that is designed to bring the brothers back to Egypt, whether Joseph really does practice divination or not. However the steward's question certainly raises the possibility.

For the Canaanites, threshing floors were where heaven met earth. But for the Israelites, the place they touched was the mercy seat on top of the Ark of the Covenant. The mercy seat was God's footstool and the cornerstone of the doorway into the heavenly realm.[159] God's name—His presence—was to be found in the cloud between the two cherubim whose wings overshadowed the Ark.

The Ark was made of acacia wood. In the Middle East acacia trees, often called *umbrella thorn* or *Israeli babool*, have a distinctive flat-topped canopy and extremely vicious spikes.[160] The acacia wood of the Ark was plated in gold, as was its lid—and that lid was the mercy seat. When the thorns were removed and the wood was enclosed in a shield of beaten gold, the result symbolised God's glory overlaying the curse of disobedience.

---

159 Many people consider a cornerstone to be one of four foundational blocks positioned where one wall meets another in a building. However, a biblical cornerstone is quite different. A biblical cornerstone is the first stone to be laid in the construction of a building. It was positioned below the doorway or the gateway and it had a shallow basin carved into it to catch any blood dripping down from the lintel or doorposts. Because the doors in biblical times were traditionally sited in the corner of a building, these stones were called cornerstones. They are part of the foundation, but have a different sense to a modern cornerstone. The placement of a biblical cornerstone set the orientation of a building. According to the traditions of Freemasonry, the orientation of the Tabernacle in the wilderness was set by Moses using two thin poles called 'asherah'. Thus in Freemasonry ritual, the deacons still carry wands with a significance originating in these 'asherah'. As the tools that set the orientation and mark the beginning for the erection of the Tabernacle, they counterfeit the cornerstone. See: lodgedevotion.net/devotion-newsletter-content/editorial-educational-articles/role-of-deacons-in-a-degree/why-do-deacons-carry-wands (accessed 7 January 2025).

160 The word for *acacia* in Hebrew basically means *turn aside*, perhaps a warning about the thorns. The city of Sodom was located in the Valley of Acacias. This was the site of the last camp of the Israelites before crossing over the Jordan under the leadership of Joshua. It was here that the people fell into sin by covenanting with Baal-Peor. The very name of the locality was perhaps a hint to them that this would be a place of testing and they would be well-advised to turn aside and camp elsewhere.

Yet Jesus is the Chief Cornerstone and therefore the true Mercy Seat. He is also the Ark of the Covenant. He is the bridge where heaven meets with earth. On resurrection day, the angels in the tomb positioned themselves over the place where He had lain just like the cherubim who covered the mercy seat—one at the head, one at the foot. Their very positioning sent the message that Jesus is the Ark with its mercy seat, and the covering for sin.

The crown of thorns is not the only reminder of the curse in this scene. So is that call of the chief priests: *'Crucify! Crucify!'* Like the thorns that pierce, so will the nails pierce, and like the thorns as the reminder of a curse, so the Cross is a reminder:

> *You must not leave the body on the tree overnight, but you must be sure to bury him that day, because anyone who is hung on a tree is under God's curse. You must not defile the land that the Lord your God is giving you as an inheritance.*
>
> Deuteronomy 21:23[BSB]

Some translations render *tree* as *pole*. This method of execution returns us once again to David's breach of covenant with the House of Saul and his grant of permission to the Gibeonites for the slaughter of Saul's descendants. The Gibeonites defiled not just the land but the Tabernacle. Instead of a blessing, they delivered a curse. Moreover, they timed the event to occur during the Passover when the greatest number of Israelites would be visiting the Tabernacle. David not only authorised the execution but allowed the defilement to continue for months.[161]

Perhaps David's covenant betrayal also involves Sychar. Was it right for him to bring the Ark of the Covenant to Jerusalem and *not* to, either:

- reunite Ark and Tabernacle at the new sanctuary of Gibeon

or

- return the Ark to its original sanctuary at Shiloh?

It's difficult to assess David's culpability, but it's certainly not zero.[162] The legitimacy of the site for the Temple rests on the identification of the location as the mountain in the land of Moriah where Abraham was prepared to sacrifice Isaac. The Samaritans disputed the claim, saying Moriah, *teacher*, was a misreading of Moreh, *teacher*, the place where Abraham had built

---

161 Once again, we see David is passive and neglectful when it comes to abuse. He did nothing about the rape of his daughter, nor did he do anything about the curse on the land (Deuteronomy 21:22–23) that he himself was instrumental in allowing. He'd asked the Gibeonites to bless the inheritance of the Lord, but they cursed the land instead and made him an accomplice to their atrocity. In addition, he does not display the justice for which the kingship should be renowned when he grants all the land Mephibosheth inherited from Saul as a reward to Mephibosheth's steward, Ziba, at the start of the civil war. On later being informed of Ziba's deception and his lies about Mephibosheth's motives in staying behind in Jerusalem, David does not return the land to its rightful owner but instead commands that it be divided between Mephibosheth and Ziba. Since Mephibosheth's remaining male relatives were all killed by the Gibeonites, David thus dispossessed the last of Saul's line of his ancestral land. He rewards the betrayer and does not stand up for those loyal to him or redress the wrongs done to them. Once again, the abusive actions of others are dumped in the 'too hard' basket and neither justice, nor restitution, nor recompense is brought to bear.

162 In installing the Tabernacle of David in the City of David, at least part of the motivation seems to be: 'Since I can't go to the Tabernacle in Gibeon as I'm too afraid, then I will set up one of my own.' At that point in the history of Israel, there were two Tabernacles—David's in Jerusalem with the Ark of the Covenant, and the original Tabernacle of Moses in Gibeon. Because of this duplication, naturally different expressions of worship grew up. Instead of animal sacrifices, the Tabernacle of David emphasised a sacrifice of praise, song, music and dance. When the Temple built by Solomon was complete, the Ark was moved into the Holy of Holies and the glory of the Lord fell on the building.

his first altar under the sacred tree near Shechem. Thus, in their view, when Abraham planned to sacrifice Isaac, he returned to the place where he'd made his very first sacrifice.

When Jesus was asked by the woman to adjudicate the place of worship—Jerusalem or Shechem—it's not simply a matter of rival mountains. Lurking in the background, there's genuine confusion about the correct labelling of the place of the Akedah[163] and, in addition, there's a churning mess of rival political motivations. Much as many people would like to think David was immune to dynastic and partisan ambitions, he simply wasn't.

So, on the one hand, the Samaritans have got a real point about Moreh and the likelihood of Abraham returning to the place of his first offering in anticipation of making his most important offering. On the other hand, the plague angel with the sword who is directed by God to, *'Withdraw your hand!'*[164] over the threshing floor of the Jebusite king—the site of the future Temple—recalls the almost-identical instruction of the angel of the Lord a thousand years previously who told Abraham to lay down his knife and not harm his son.

Jesus' comment on the right place for worship indicated that both Jerusalem and Shechem are correct and both are also incorrect. Here, once again, we see Jesus healing history. God was always meant to tabernacle amongst His people, not to be confined to a Temple in Jerusalem, nor to a sanctuary in Shiloh or Gibeon, nor to a sacred precinct on top of Mount Gerizim. It's not wrong to worship God in any of those places, but it *is* wrong to suggest that no other place is legitimate.

---

163 Jewish term meaning *binding* that traditionally refers to the testing of Abraham. It denotes the binding of Isaac.
164 2 Samuel 24:16[NIV]

The Temple was David's idea, not God's. God made it clear it was not His desire, but He conceded to David's wishes—at least in part. He gave approval for David's successor to build it.

It's not in a building made of hands but in Spirit and in Truth that God desires worship.

6.6 The Covenant

Many Samaritans from that town believed in Him because of the woman's testimony, 'He told me all that I ever did.' So when the Samaritans came to Him, they asked Him to stay with them, and He stayed there two days. And many more believed because of His word.

They said to the woman, 'It is no longer because of what you said that we believe, for we have heard for ourselves, and we know that this is indeed the Saviour of the world.'

John 4:39–42^{ESV}

The Jewish leaders insisted, 'We have a law, and according to that law He must die, because He claimed to be the Son of God.'

John 19:7^{NIV}

AT THIS POINT IN THE NARRATIVE of the fourth chapter we should become alert to the fact this is no ordinary woman. If she is, as many people today think, five times divorced with such an unsavoury reputation that she can't even associate with other women of her town, why would anyone listen to her? And, even if they did, why would they drop every racial and cultural barrier that had been built up over centuries to ask a Jew to stay, just on her say-so? Where is the natural disbelief, the nudge-nudge-wink-wink sure-sure yeah-right reaction? Why didn't the people need more than just, *'He told me all that I ever did,'* in order to overcome the Everest-high walls of prejudice and contemptuous hatred that existed between the Samaritans and the Jews? Where's the skepticism, the doubt, the distrust and mistrust?

This is no ordinary invitation. Even today, to ask a stranger, a potential enemy, to stay would be abnormal but, in the past, because an offer of covenant is necessarily involved, it's beyond extraordinary. Right up until the end of the nineteenth century—and sometimes even now in parts of the Middle East—to ask someone to stay implies that they will step over the cornerstone under the doorway of a house and, through that simple action, to covenant with the host. Yes, *covenant*. On the strength of the woman's testimony, the Samaritans not only offered Jesus hospitality, they invited Him into *oneness* with them—the *oneness* of threshold covenant.[165] They were, in fact, enacting a Passover ritual—for the blood on the lintels and doorposts at the Passover is simply the sign of an invitation to God to accept the covenant and *pass over* the cornerstone,[166] be the Guest of the household, and accept the obligations of mutual defence should the need arise.

---

[165] Also called *cornerstone covenant*. The oneness of threshold covenant can be expressed in these terms: *I will defend you to the death if this house is attacked. My weapons are as your weapons. Your fight is my fight.* Another way of enacting this covenant, other than by passing over the stone in the doorway, was to exchange weapons. This is what happened with David and Jonathan. David was therefore obligated, when he knew the Philistines were about to attack the armies of Saul and Jonathan, to go to their aid. That is why he used the ephod: he wanted God to make the decision as to whether he should rescue the families of his men or attend to his covenantal obligations.

[166] The opposite of *passing over* was *stumbling* or *striking* or *dashing a foot* against the cornerstone. It indicated that the invitation to the feast and to be an overnight guest was declined and that covenant was refused.

Jesus, as the Son of God, accepts this Passover-like request. This is huge—for both hosts and Guest. In the town where covenant reaffirmation was such an enormous aspect of the local history, the people raise a covenant with Jesus. His is the sixth, or seventh, major covenant to be enacted here. The count depends on whether we include the coronation of Rehoboam in the list or not. Since seventh would be such a significant symbol of completeness, perhaps we can assume that Rehoboam's coronation was included.

These historic covenants parallel the marriages of the woman of Samaria. She perfectly represents the land. Now, as Isaiah tells us, the land is to be married to the king, to God Himself:

> *The Lord will take delight in you, and your land will be married.*
>
> *As a young man marries a young woman, so will your Builder marry you; as a bridegroom rejoices over his bride, so will your God rejoice over you.*
>
> Isaiah 62:4–5^{NIV}

So Jesus, at Sychar, has to marry the land by covenanting with the Samaritans. As we read the Scriptural passage today, there's seemingly no evidence of that. We'd like an explicit statement to that effect in the text. But that's to miss the customs of the time. We're simply told Jesus stayed with them for two days. That means He ate and drank with them and went into their homes. This acceptance of hospitality necessarily entailed taking part in a threshold covenant.

Now, on listening to Jesus over two days, the Samaritans concluded the woman was right. They transferred their faith in her testimony to faith in Jesus Himself and decided He was the 'Saviour of the World'.

No higher compliment could have been paid by the Samaritans. They were comparing Him to Joseph, the son of Jacob, whose tomb was nearby. 'Saviour of the World' is one of the possible alternative translations of Zaphenath-Paneah, the name Pharaoh gave to Joseph. Joseph was the ancestor of the tribe of Ephraim and this area was the hill country of Ephraim. The people might have been brought in from Kutha and other cities of the Assyrian Empire but they intermarried with the tribe of Ephraim. So the title they gave to Jesus meant that they saw Him at least on a level with the most revered of their forefathers.

The breach between peoples that was caused by Rehoboam has been healed: the kingdom of David has been restored to a unified whole, on earth. In heaven, it had always been united through an everlasting covenant in the Person of Jesus, just as God had promised. Yet it's so different from what anyone expected, Pilate couldn't understand it. How could he? If the Jewish people didn't get it, how could anyone else? The inviolable kingdom of heaven isn't built on power but on self-sacrificial love.

The facilitator of all this reunification was a woman. We can be almost certain she wasn't divorced. Only the wealthiest of women could initiate a marital split; it was almost always a sole male prerogative. If it had happened even once, the woman would have found it virtually impossible to marry again. No man would have even thought to approach her. But if she had been widowed, it would have been an entirely different story. A near relative, most likely the brother of her deceased husband, would have married her to fulfil the obligations of Levirate marriage. Her situation may well have been closely paralleled by the scenario the Sadducees posed to Jesus to try to test and trap Him:

> *Now some Sadducees, who claim there is no resurrection, came to Jesus and asked Him, 'Teacher, Moses wrote for us that if a man's brother dies and leaves a wife but no child, the man should marry the widow and have children for his brother. Now there were seven brothers. The first one married and died childless. Then the second and the third married her. In the same way, all seven died and left no children. Finally, the woman died, too. Now in the resurrection, whose wife will the woman be, since the seven had married her?'*
>
> Luke 20:27–33[ISV]

If this is the woman's story, it is one of heart-wrenching tragedy. Her final situation was apparently living under the roof of a kinsman of her five husbands who, for some reason, either could not marry her or else, thinking much the same as Judah when he withheld his youngest son from Tamar,[167] was not willing to risk the outcome. It might have been a matter of compromising an inheritance, as detailed in the Book of Ruth. Or the widow might not be too dissimilar to Sarah, the heroine of the apocryphal Book of Tobit, whose seven husbands were killed on the wedding night by the demon Asmodeus.

John Loren Sandford suggests that, by the time several of her husbands had died, the woman would have been considered a prophet. Obviously she was not the Taheb, the prophet-like-Moses, but nonetheless she would be a woman of some status in the community. Her word would not have been taken lightly but considered to be oracular in nature. This, after all, was Sychar where Jacob dug his well and Abraham had built that first altar

---

167 Judah thought Tamar was cursed and didn't want to risk his youngest son dying as the two older ones had. See: Genesis 38:11.

under the Great Oak of Moreh, *the tree of the teacher* or *the oracular, speaking, tree.*[168]

Her word would thus command the instant attention of prophecy. If she said the Messiah had come, then people would rush to see for themselves.

In the contrasting chiastic section, the bias and unbelief of the Jewish leaders is juxtaposed with the ardent belief and covenantal loyalty of the Samaritans. The world had turned upside down—it should have been the Samaritans who were bigoted and narrow-minded, not the Jews.

John does not record any miracles done in Sychar. Apparently the Samaritans were convinced simply by hearing Jesus speak. Like Mary at Cana and like the royal official whose story follows on from Jesus' visit to Samaria, the people of Sychar did not need signs.[169] All of them committed themselves to belief in the 'logos', the *word*, of Jesus and in Him as the Logos. And perhaps because they didn't ask for signs before acting in faith, they received what they desired.

However for the chief priests and most of the Sanhedrin, the signs and wonders, the stunning miracles done in their very midst, were not enough. It wasn't as if Jesus had confined His healing to Galilee and the lands beyond the Jordan. He'd cured a man born

---

168 The oak (or terebinth) of Moreh, the 'elon moreh' is translated *oracle tree* by Thomas Mann. This is a reminder of El's oracle (that is, Bull El, the elder-god of the Canaanite pantheon, not Yahweh) and of Baal's promise regarding it to reveal the word of tree and whisper of stone to Anat at Zaphon. Significantly, once again, we are dealing with counterfeits and antitypes to heavenly truth. Rabbi Jesus, the Teacher and the Son of David, of whom Solomon is a faint and flawed foreshadowing is the true oracle of the Holy Spirit.

169 Mary is presented in John's gospel as the first person to make a radical commitment of faith to the word proclaimed by Jesus.

blind in Jerusalem itself near the Pool of Siloam[170] and a lame man at the Pool of Bethesda, near the Sheep Gate.[171] It wasn't as if these healings were discreet—they were seriously controversial because both had occurred on the Sabbath.

By His actions, Jesus was making a statement and it was much more profound than anything about the Sabbath. Back a thousand years, before the fortress of Zion had been conquered and renamed the City of David, the Jebusites had taunted David's armies, saying even the blind and the lame could ward them off.[172] Taking the hint, a detachment of soldiers crawled up a dark water channel into the allegedly impregnable stronghold.

By curing the blind and the lame, Jesus was proclaiming that anyone could enter into His inviolable kingdom—anyone at all. It wasn't just for the able-bodied, for the wealthy, for the racially pure, or solely for the male of the species. It was for everyone.

And to make it as simple as possible, so that even the smallest child could enter the kingdom, all that would ever be required as a covenantal obligation was believing trust—believing trust in Himself as the Son of God and Saviour of the World.

170　John 9:1–7
171　John 5:1–9
172　2 Samuel 5:6

6.7 Symbols of Covenant

> *And He said to him, 'I am the Lord who brought you out of Ur of the Chaldeans, to give you this land to possess it.'*
> *But he said, 'Lord God, how may I know that I will possess it?'*
> *So He said to him, 'Bring Me a three-year-old heifer, a three-year-old female goat, a three-year-old ram, a turtledove, and a young pigeon.*
> *Then he brought all these to Him and cut them in two, and laid each half opposite the other…*
>
> Genesis 15:7–10^{NASB}

Abram *cuts*[173] his first covenant with God—a blood covenant, as opposed to a name, threshold, salt or peace covenant—by providing three three-year-old animals and two birds for a sacrifice. The animals are cut in half, symbolising the willingness of the covenant partners to die for each other and also symbolising the penalty for betrayal of the covenant. Between the separated parts of the animals was a pool of blood through which the participants would walk in a figure-of-eight, reciting the blessings and curses.

The division of the creatures into two halves as emblematic of a profession of covenant was probably behind the specific

---

[173] The technical word for making covenant was to *cut* a covenant, because of the cut pieces of sacrifice. However, if a covenant was with God, the term could also be to *raise* a covenant.

directions given by Moses as to how the Israelites were to reaffirm their covenant with God once they reached the Promised Land:

> *Then Moses and the elders of Israel commanded the people: 'Keep all the commandments I am giving you today. And on the day you cross the Jordan into the land that the Lord your God is giving you, set up large stones and coat them with plaster. Write on them all the words of this law ... you are to set up these stones on Mount Ebal, as I am commanding you today, and you are to coat them with plaster.'*
>
> *... On that day Moses commanded the people: 'When you have crossed the Jordan, these tribes shall stand on Mount Gerizim to bless the people: Simeon, Levi, Judah, Issachar, Joseph, and Benjamin. And these tribes shall stand on Mount Ebal to deliver the curse: Reuben, Gad, Asher, Zebulun, Dan, and Naphtali.'*
>
> Deuteronomy 27:1–4;11–13^{BSB}

Mount Ebal and Mount Gerizim, with Shechem in the valley between, provided a picture of covenant in the landscape: two heights divided with a cut between. It was a place that imaged the two halves of a covenant sacrifice.

Perhaps the chiastic structure of John's gospel with its mirror division between front and back is designed with this covenantal imagery in mind. Perhaps, in fact, the use of chiasmus throughout all Hebrew prophecy and poetry is meant to evoke the two halves of covenant. John's gospel is perhaps structured, according to the commands of Moses, in an Ebal-Gerizim fashion with blessings pronounced on the one hand and curses on the other.

The very first city built by a descendant of Abraham in the land that would become the inheritance of the Israelites had a covenantal pattern. Sheerah, the daughter of Ephraim and granddaughter of Joseph, built her city in two parts. At the bottom of a steep narrow incline was Lower Beth Horon and at the top was Upper Beth Horon. Throughout the entire history of Israel from the time of Joshua to that of the Jewish war with Rome, the Hebrews never lost a battle fought on that hillside. Joshua contended with five armies there and it was at this location he famously called on the sun and the moon to stand still.

The name 'horon' can have several meanings including *hollow* or *cave*. However it is also the name of an Egyptian deity usually coupled in worship with Resheph and Anat.

Joshua's battle, a conflict that involved him summoning time to do his bidding as Jesus did at Cana—since his command for the sun and moon to stand still was, in reality, a call for more time to finish the battle before his opponents could escape—was against the spiritual forces behind the Canaanites. Their patron at the time was Anat, the berserker war-goddess. In the epic that describes her battles, she is continually described as wading in blood between two villages or between two tables or between the east and the west.[174]

She is apparently stepping in a covenant-like space where the pool of blood should be in order to wreak havoc there. It would appear her battle lust is not sated until she has not just slaughtered everyone she encounters but has also disrupted covenant in the process. The purpose of covenant is defence, not war. It's about the promotion of peace and security, not bloodshed.

Jesus chooses the place carefully and provocatively to combat Anat and her allies. He deliberately raises a covenant of defence in the vicinity of Joseph's tomb in a valley between two mountains. In doing so, He establishes His right to be both king of the world and its saviour.

---

174 See: sumerianlanguage.tumblr.com/post/165307767415/baal-and-anat-ktu-13i-iii (accessed 11 December 2024)

6.8 I Cannot Tell

I cannot tell why He, whom angels worship,
should set His love upon the sons of men,
or why, as Shepherd, He should seek the wanderers,
to bring them back, they know not how or when.
But this I know, that He was born of Mary
when Bethl'em's manger was His only home,
and that He lived at Nazareth and laboured,
and so the Saviour, Saviour of the world, is come.

I cannot tell how silently He suffered,
as with His peace He graced this place of tears,
or how His heart upon the cross was broken,
the crown of pain to three and thirty years.
But this I know, He heals the broken-hearted
and stays our sin and calms our lurking fear
and lifts the burden from the heavy laden;
for still the Saviour, Saviour of the world is here.

I cannot tell how He will win the nations,
how He will claim His earthly heritage,
how satisfy the needs and aspirations
of east and west, of sinner and of sage.
But this I know, all flesh shall see His glory,
and He shall reap the harvest He has sown,
and some glad day His sun will shine in splendour
when He the Saviour, Saviour of the world, is known.

I cannot tell how all the lands shall worship,
when at His bidding every storm is stilled,
or who can say how great the jubilation
when every heart with love and joy is filled.
But this I know, the skies will thrill with rapture,
and myriad myriad human voices sing,
and earth to heav'n, and heav'n to earth, will answer,
'At last the Saviour, Saviour of the world, is King!'

WY Fullerton

PART

After the two days He departed for Galilee. (For Jesus Himself had testified that a prophet has no honour in his own hometown.) So when He came to Galilee, the Galileans welcomed Him, having seen all that He had done in Jerusalem at the feast. For they too had gone to the feast.

So He came again to Cana in Galilee, where He had made the water wine. And at Capernaum there was an official whose son was ill. When this man heard that Jesus had come from Judea to Galilee, he went to Him and asked Him to come down and heal his son, for he was at the point of death.

So Jesus said to him, 'Unless you see signs and wonders you will not believe.'

The official said to Him, 'Sir, come down before my child dies.'

Jesus said to him, 'Go; your son will live.'

The man believed the word that Jesus spoke to him and went on his way. As he was going down, his servants met him and told him that his son was recovering. So he asked them the hour when he began to get better, and they said to him, 'Yesterday at the seventh hour the fever left him.'

The father knew that was the hour when Jesus had said to him, 'Your son will live.' And he himself believed, and all his household. This was now the second sign that Jesus did when He had come from Judea to Galilee.

John 4:43–54 ESV

SEVEN

When Pilate heard this, he was even more afraid, and he went back inside the palace. 'Where do you come from?' he asked Jesus, but Jesus gave him no answer. 'Do You refuse to speak to me?' Pilate said. 'Don't You realise I have power either to free You or to crucify You?'

Jesus answered, 'You would have no power over Me if it were not given to you from above. Therefore the one who handed Me over to you is guilty of a greater sin.'

From then on, Pilate tried to set Jesus free, but the Jewish leaders kept shouting, 'If you let this man go, you are no friend of Caesar. Anyone who claims to be a king opposes Caesar.'

John 19:8–12 NIV

7.1 The Trap

> *When Pilate heard this, he was even more afraid, and he went back inside the palace. 'Where do you come from?' he asked Jesus, but Jesus gave him no answer. 'Do You refuse to speak to me?' Pilate said. 'Don't You realise I have power either to free You or to crucify You?'*
>
> John 19:8–10[NIV]

THE CHIEF PRIESTS HAD CHOSEN their words carefully. They didn't describe Jesus as 'the Messiah' but as the 'Son of God'.

The trap was sprung. For the Romans, this title had originated with Augustus Caesar who, on the deification of his adoptive father Julius, styled himself 'Divi Filius', *son of a god*. Augustus' successor, Tiberius, also used the title, as later did Nero and Domitian.

The chief priests obviously thought that, by presenting Jesus as a rival to the Emperor Tiberius, they had manipulated Pilate into a corner where he had no option but to condemn Jesus. But this was not necessarily the case. Pilate may have understood that what Jesus was claiming was not religious status but family status. His words could have been interpreted as a claim to be related to the emperor. No wonder Pilate was afraid.

The political situation in Rome was so volatile that a hitherto-unknown heir to the empire would not necessarily have been regarded in an adversarial light. He might even have been welcomed effusively, depending on whose son he was. The emperor Tiberius, having fallen into a despondent state and retired to the Isle of Capri after the death of his son Drusus and nephew Germanicus, would almost certainly have been delighted to find a long-lost relative. If Jesus really happened to be an illegitimate grandson of Tiberius, the mood of the entire empire probably would change for the better. The strongman, Sejanus, who had consolidated his power in Tiberius' absence and whose tyrannical rule caused widespread terror would no longer be in control.

So Pilate is in a double bind—and he desperately needs more information about Jesus. What are His origins? Where does He come from? Who is His father?

Pilate would have realised he was making the most critical decision of his life: if he signed the death warrant for Caesar's heir—and it was ever found out—he wouldn't survive the fallout. But if Jesus is a fraud, and he let Him live so that He rose to become a serious rival to the power of Rome, he wouldn't survive that fallout either.

Potentially there are two rival kings: Jesus and Caesar.

Jesus is simply not answering questions about His origins. Why should He? It's irrelevant to His guilt or innocence and Pilate already knows that.

7.2 The Route and the Time

After the two days He departed for Galilee. (For Jesus Himself had testified that a prophet has no honour in his own hometown.) So when He came to Galilee, the Galileans welcomed Him, having seen all that He had done in Jerusalem at the feast. For they too had gone to the feast.

John 4:43–45^{ESV}

Jesus tended to stay two days at places before moving on the third day. In the opening chapter of the gospel, John the Baptiser identifies Jesus as the 'Lamb of God' to his followers. Jesus then remained for two days at Bethany-beyond-the-Jordan before returning to Galilee. Later, when Jesus is once again at Bethany-beyond-the-Jordan and receives the news of Lazarus' illness, He famously waits two more days before setting off.

Here, at Sychar, He spends two days with the Samaritans before He moves on once again.

Now just as the towns along their travels from Bethany-beyond-the-Jordan to Cana turned out to be significant for the events at the wedding,[175] so once again the towns en route from Sychar

---

175 See: *The Summoning of Time*, the second volume in this series.

The Inviolable Kingdom

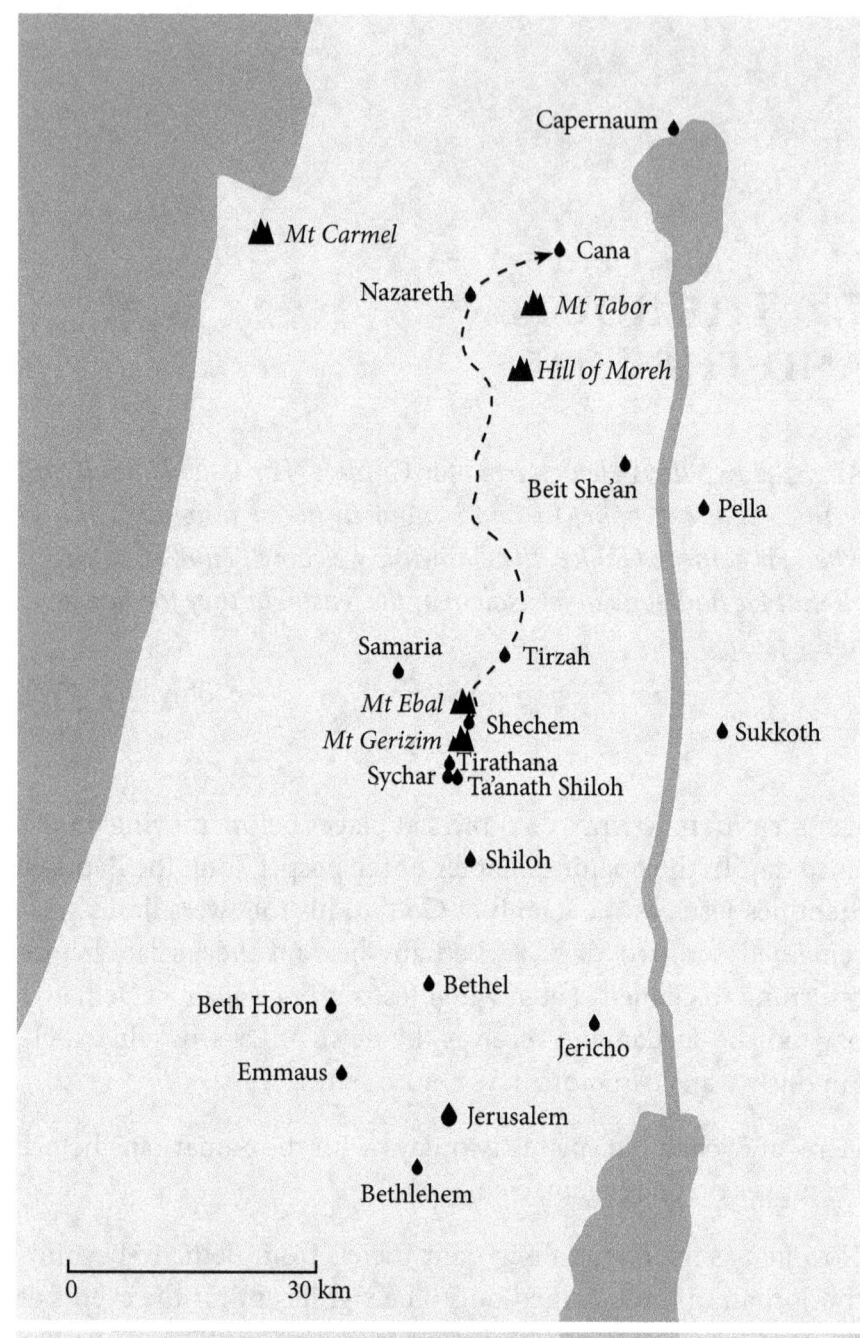

Route of Jesus

to Cana are significant for what happens with the royal official. The band of the Twelve[176] with Jesus at their head journeys on through the Pass of Shechem with the mountains of blessing and cursing—Gerizim and Ebal—on either side. Then it's on through Tirzah, another early capital of the northern kingdom. It was only in the days of Omri, the father of Ahab, that the capital shifted to the hill of Samaria. Under the breakaway rule of Jeroboam, Shechem was the first leading city of the new kingdom before Tirzah was established as Jeroboam's base.

Now the Samaritans had welcomed Jesus. The Galileans also welcomed Jesus. The comment by John that Jesus had said a prophet never has honour in his own hometown implies that, not only had a surprising change occurred, but that their journey took them through Nazareth before veering off to Cana. Apparently Jesus' stay in Sychar meant that His neighbours in Nazareth had got back to Galilee ahead of Him after the feast in Jerusalem and spread the word. John isn't clear what feast Jesus had attended and he hasn't told us what Jesus did there to change the attitude of the Galileans towards Him. All he reported at the beginning of the chapter was that Jesus had made the decision to return to Galilee on discovering that the Pharisees were tallying the count of those His disciples baptised compared with the followers of John the Baptiser. It seems that He learned this during the feast.

Although no direct information is given, I believe that the interaction between Jesus and the Samaritan woman occurred either during, or alternatively in the lead-up to, the Feast of Tabernacles. The reason I hold this view is because their discussion revolves around 'Living Water'—and that happens to be the theme of three other major incidents that occur during Tabernacles in the different years throughout Jesus' ministry. It simply fits the

---

176 We have to assume it's 12 by this stage though John hasn't actually informed us of any additions to the first five.

pattern. In the three-and-a-half years Jesus was active, there were, according to my reckoning, four Feasts of Tabernacles and, on those occasions, Jesus was first at Cana, then at Sychar/Cana, third at Jerusalem and lastly on top of Mount Hermon.

Assuming my deduction is correct, then the unspecified feast John refers to would have been Yom Kippur, the Day of Atonement. Jesus and His disciples were in Jerusalem for that occasion, and they intended to return to Galilee in time for the week-long Feast of Tabernacles, six days later. This timeframe links us straight back into the opening of the gospel when John the Baptiser was quizzed about his identity on the Day of Atonement. Jesus then turned up the next day and stayed for another, before heading off to Cana with five newly-minted followers. They arrived in time for a wedding being held over the week of the Feast of Tabernacles.

Assuming that I have correctly identified the feast John is referencing, then even with the delay, Jesus would be returning to Cana in the middle of Tabernacles for the anniversary of His first miracle—His first 'sign', as John puts it. It seems He was visiting the newlyweds after their first year of marriage. This was a significant time in Jewish tradition because of the Torah injunction:

> *When a man has taken a new wife, he shall not go out to war or be charged with any business; he shall be free at home one year, and bring happiness to his wife whom he has taken.*
>
> Deuteronomy 24:5[NKJV]

It's a time of transition for both the husband and the wife—who was probably Jesus' sister—and it would be natural in His care for her to seek the couple out during this time.

7.3 Origins

(For Jesus Himself had testified that a prophet has no honour in his own hometown.) So when He came to Galilee, the Galileans welcomed Him...

John 4:44–45^{ESV}

When Pilate heard this, he was even more afraid, and he went back inside the palace. 'Where do you come from?' he asked Jesus, but Jesus gave him no answer.

John 19: 8–9^{NIV}

UNEXPECTEDLY, THE GALILEANS WELCOMED JESUS, just as the Samaritans had. Pilate was in a dilemma wondering whether or not he should welcome Jesus. The title 'Son of God' wasn't a spiritual predicament for him as much as a political one. The chief priests, however, were completely unwelcoming of Jesus and tried to corral Pilate against his best instincts into the outcome they wanted.

The answer to Pilate's anxious question, *'Where do you come from?'*, is provided in John's chiastic parallel: Jesus' hometown is in Galilee. A prophet might be honoured in virtually every community other than where he grew up, but the exception to that rule is Jerusalem:

> 'O Jerusalem, Jerusalem, the city that kills the prophets and stones God's messengers! How often I have wanted to gather your children together as a hen protects her chicks beneath her wings, but you wouldn't let Me.'
>
> Matthew 23:37^{NLT}

That declaration of Jesus that Jerusalem is the city that murders God's messengers will be fulfilled yet again in His own death.

7.4 Prophets and Kings

> *So He came again to Cana in Galilee, where He had made the water wine. And at Capernaum there was an official whose son was ill. When this man heard that Jesus had come from Judea to Galilee, he went to Him and asked Him to come down and heal his son, for he was at the point of death.*
>
> John 4:46–47 ESV

> *Jesus answered, 'You would have no power over Me if it were not given to you from above. Therefore the one who handed Me over to you is guilty of a greater sin.'*
>
> John 19:11 NIV

Although the idea has fallen out of favour in recent times, back in the nineteenth century it was thought that the official who came to seek help from Jesus was Chuza, the steward of King Herod mentioned in Luke's gospel.[177] I believe that identification is correct based on the very faint hints running through the background to the story. The Greek word used by John to describe the official is 'basilikos', *little king* or *petty king*. Different translations render this as *royal official, nobleman, courtier*. Since the man comes from Capernaum, he obviously belongs to the household of Herod Antipas, tetrarch of Galilee and Perea. He is also described as an 'epitrophos', *chief-of-staff*.

---

177 Luke 8:3

Herod Antipas was of Idumean descent. His first wife, Phasa'el, was the daughter of Aretas IV, the Nabataean king of Arabia centred on Petra. She'd been divorced by Antipas so he could marry Herodias, the wife of his half-brother Herod Philip.[178] This marital shuffle had been denounced by John the Baptiser and, as a consequence of making an enemy of Herodias, John was eventually beheaded.

Chuza is a Nabataean name, meaning *seer* or *visionary*.[179] It would not have been out of place for Antipas to appoint as a steward of his estates a business manager who had Gentile ancestry similar to his own and who, moreover, came from the same place as his first wife. In designating the official as a *little king*, John demonstrates that this episode is closely linked in with the reunification-of-the-kingdom theme begun in the account of the Samaritan woman and confirmed by the continuing dialogue about kingship and authority between Pilate and Jesus. In addition, both the Samaritan woman and Chuza may have been prophets. The meaning of his name suggests that possibility.

Recall that David's kingdom was split between two rivals: Rehoboam and Jeroboam. But long before the kingdom ripped apart, David's royal mantle had already been symbolically shredded by the prophet Ahijah from Shiloh.

> *Jeroboam was an able young man, and when Solomon noticed how hard he worked, he put him in charge of all the forced labour in the territory of the tribes of Manasseh and Ephraim. One day, as Jeroboam was travelling from Jerusalem, the prophet Ahijah from Shiloh met him alone on the road in the open country. Ahijah took off the new robe he was wearing, tore it into twelve pieces, and said to*

---

178 Not to be confused with Philip the Tetrarch, who was Herod Philip II.
179 See: abarim-publications.com/Meaning/Chuza.html (accessed 22 October 2024)

> *Jeroboam, 'Take ten pieces for yourself, because the Lord, the God of Israel, says to you, "I am going to take the kingdom away from Solomon, and I will give you ten tribes. Solomon will keep one tribe for the sake of My servant David and for the sake of Jerusalem, the city I have chosen to be My own from the whole land of Israel."'*
>
> 1 Kings 11:28–32^{GNT}

Now it's clear that the unnamed chief executive who approaches Jesus to heal his son is meant to evoke Jeroboam. My reasons for identifying him as Chuza are based on the following parallels:

- Jeroboam was a royal official, just as Chuza was.
- Jeroboam was the son of Nebat, and Chuza was a son of 'Nabatu', the name the Nabataeans had for themselves.[180]
- One possible translation of both Nebat and Chuza is *behold*.
- Jeroboam meets a prophet who has come from Shiloh, and Chuza meets the prophet-like-Moses who has just come from Shiloh.
- Jeroboam was married to a foreigner—after he fled to Egypt when Solomon discovered the prophecy and tried to kill him.[181] He married the sister-in-law of Pharaoh Shishak.[182] Likewise, Chuza was married to a woman foreign to his own ethnicity—a Jewish woman named

---

[180] The name 'Nabatu' means *people who draw water*. Here we have a link both into the story of the Samaritan woman who was asked to draw water for Jesus but to the mantle of Moses, the prophet who was named for being drawn from the water.

[181] Echoes of the story of Herod the Great and Jesus.

[182] Her name is thought to be Ano, possibly related to Anat.

Joanna.[183] She became a major benefactor of Jesus' ministry. Her strong financial support must have been authorised by her husband. She is named in Luke's gospel as one of the witnesses to the resurrection.

- Jeroboam was supported by a foreign king. Jesus, indirectly through Joanna and Chuza who was paid by Herod, was also supported by a foreign king.

Jeroboam led an uprising against Rehoboam. He was a rebel and a revolutionary. There's no insurrectionist in the story of the healing of the royal official's son, but there is one in the parallel account featuring the murderer and insurgent, Barabbas.

Barabbas' name is not in a perfect mirror position but it is within the scope of the wider chiastic block. Barabbas in fact forms the link between the Samaritan woman and the 'little king', unifying their stories. The official's story harks back to that of an overseer of former times who became a revolutionary: Jeroboam.

However, there's a much more significant pointer to Jeroboam than simply these parallels between two administrators in different time periods accused of sedition against the state. It's all about the boy.

---

183 She too appears to be of high status and is regarded by some commentators as belonging to the high priestly family of Annas. It is known that a granddaughter of Theophilus, who was the son of Annas, as well as high priest from 37–41 AD, and who may be the addressee of Luke's gospel, was called Joanna. However, the date does not seem to fit any granddaughter. However, if the granddaughter was named after an aunt, it would fit. Only Luke mentions Joanna (twice) but he does so in a very significant way. A small poem at the end of Luke's gospel has her name prominently displayed as a witness to the resurrection at the very centre of a chiastic structure.

7.5 Prophets and Authorities

Some commentators, on noting the similarity between the story of Jesus healing the servant boy of the centurion from Capernaum and this episode of the son of the royal official, think they refer to the same event.

No. One is about the nature of authority, the other is about the healing of history. In the case of the centurion's servant, there are several linked stories that culminate in a demonstration that the authority of Jesus is much superior to that of Caesar as the lord of the legions. In the case of the official's son, there is a recapitulation of the illness of Jeroboam's son—but, naturally, with a different ending.

> *At that time Abijah, son of Jeroboam, got sick. Jeroboam told his wife, 'Go to Shiloh, but disguise yourself so that people will not recognise you as my wife. The prophet Ahijah, who told me I would be king of these people, is there. Take ten loaves of bread, some raisins, and a jar of honey with you, and go to him. He will tell you what will happen to the boy.'*

Jeroboam's wife did this. She left, went to Shiloh, and came to the home of Ahijah. Ahijah couldn't see. His eyesight had failed because he was old. However, the Lord had told Ahijah, 'Jeroboam's wife is coming to ask you about her son who is sick. When she comes, she will pretend to be someone else.' He also told Ahijah what to say to her.

Ahijah heard her footsteps when she came into the room. He said, 'Come in. You're Jeroboam's wife. Why are you pretending to be someone else? I've been told to give you some terrible news. Tell Jeroboam, "This is what the Lord God of Israel says: I picked you out of the people and made you a leader over My people Israel. I tore the kingdom away from David's heirs and gave it to you. But you have not been like My servant David. He obeyed My commands and faithfully followed Me by doing only what I considered right. You have done more evil things than everyone before you. You made other gods, metal idols, for yourself. You made Me furious and turned your back to Me. That is why I will bring disaster on Jeroboam's house. I will destroy every male in his house, whether slave or freeman in Israel. I will burn down Jeroboam's house. It will burn like manure until it is gone. If anyone from Jeroboam's house dies in the city, dogs will eat him. If anyone dies in the country, birds will eat him."

'The Lord has said this! Get up, and go home. The moment you set foot in the city the child will die. All Israel will mourn for him and bury him. He is the only one of Jeroboam's family who will be properly buried. He was the only one in Jeroboam's house in whom the Lord God of Israel found anything good. The Lord will appoint a king over Israel. That king will destroy Jeroboam's house. This will happen today. It will happen right now.

'The Lord will strike Israel like cattails which shake in the water. He will uproot Israel from this good land which He gave their ancestors. He will scatter them beyond the Euphrates River because they dedicated poles to the goddess Asherah and made the Lord furious. So the Lord will desert Israel because of Jeroboam's sins, the sins which he led Israel to commit."

Jeroboam's wife got up, left, and went to Tirzah. When she walked across the threshold of her home, the boy died. All Israel buried him and mourned for him as the Lord had said through His servant, the prophet Ahijah.

1 Kings 14:1–18^{GWT}

There's a sweeping generalisation here about how David always obeyed the Lord's commandments that seems more like it's the prophet's wishful thinking than God's words. It wouldn't be the first time a prophet has done a bit of spin-doctoring on what God has said. For example, in Numbers 25:4 God tells Moses to round up the *ringleaders* responsible for worshipping Baal-Peor and execute them. In the next verse, Numbers 25:5, Moses issues orders to kill *everyone* involved.[184]

---

184 Another time Moses misquotes God is at Sinai. God tells him to inform the people to consecrate themselves, wash their clothes, and not approach the mountain. Moses relays the third item in this list by telling the men to refrain from sex with their wives. (Exodus 19:10–15) He also reports past events in the first chapter of Deuteronomy in such a way as to suggest he's forgotten what happened or that he's trying to rewrite history. He doesn't mention his father-in-law Jethro as the source of the idea to appoint leaders to hear minor disputes so he would not be burdened by judging every case. Instead, he gives himself the credit (Deuteronomy 1:9–18 vs Exodus 18:13–26). Once again, he makes a mis-attribution when he says in Deuteronomy 1:22 that the people came up with the notion to send out spies to scout the land and it seemed a good idea to Moses, whereas Numbers 13:1 tells us the spies were sent out at Yahweh's direction. In this same speech, Moses claims the words of Caleb and Joshua were spoken by himself.

God tells us to weigh the words of the prophets carefully.[185] Even with a genuine prophet, we may need to sift the grain from the chaff. Sometimes, the messenger gets in the way of the message. So let's not view Ahijah's words as unadulterated truth.

When we compare this story about Jeroboam's wife with that of Jesus being approached by the official, we see both immediate similarities and differences. A child is dying. But in the time of Jesus it is not the wife who travels to the prophet for a word, it is the husband. Perhaps that's what Jeroboam should have done: humbled himself to go and ask for healing for his son, repented of his pride and idolatry, been grateful for his elevation to kingship and turned back to God. Yet it's the old, old story. Power corrupts and absolute power tends to corrupt absolutely.

Now, just as the wife is unnamed in Jeroboam's story, so is the royal official—though, as I've pointed out, I believe he can be identified as Chuza. And if that is correct, then both Jeroboam's wife and Chuza are foreigners—she was Egyptian and had come from Pharaoh's court, he was Nabataean and came from Herod's court.

> *So Jesus said to him, 'Unless you see signs and wonders you will not believe.'*
>
> *The official said to Him, 'Sir, come down before my child dies.'*
>
> *Jesus said to him, 'Go; your son will live.'*
>
> *The man believed the word that Jesus spoke to him and went on his way.*
>
> John 4:48–50[ESV]

Just as the word was given to Jeroboam's wife that her son would die and she left, so now the word is given to the official and he left.

---

185   1 Corinthians 14:29.

Perhaps he'd heard about the centurion whose servant had been healed, just because Jesus had given the word. It's more than likely he had—after all, the centurion was based in Capernaum.

> *When He entered Capernaum, a centurion came to Him asking for help: 'Lord, my servant is lying at home paralysed, in terrible anguish.'*
>
> *Jesus said to him, 'I will come and heal him.'*
>
> *But the centurion replied, 'Lord, I am not worthy to have You come under my roof. Instead, just say the word and my servant will be healed. For I too am a man under authority, with soldiers under me. I say to this one, "Go" and he goes, and to another "Come" and he comes, and to my slave "Do this" and he does it.'*
>
> *When Jesus heard this He was amazed and said to those who followed Him, 'I tell you the truth, I have not found such faith in anyone in Israel!...' Then Jesus said to the centurion, 'Go; just as you believed, it will be done for you.' And the servant was healed at that hour.*
>
> Matthew 8:5–13^{NET}

Now it may even have been this centurion's suggestion that Chuza seek out Jesus and appeal for help. After all, if Jesus had been willing to respond to his plea—that of a Roman soldier of the occupying forces of Galilee—surely He'd be even more willing to help one of the local ruler's most trusted servants—wouldn't He? The centurion possibly persuaded Chuza he had nothing to lose and everything to gain.

Apparently Chuza remembered the statement of the centurion about lines of authority and he simply believed Jesus and went back the way he came. The King of kings had spoken and so His command would be obeyed and His will made manifest, at once, by His servants in the spiritual realm.

This was the lesson the centurion had taught all the people of Israel. By saying he was a man under authority, he was putting his position in context. At the pinnacle of the empire, the emperor made known his will and immediately, acting on his authority, an entire hierarchy of servants put in train all that was necessary to bring the emperor's desire to fruition. The centurion himself was part of that hierarchy—he received orders from his superiors and then directed those under him accordingly. In Jesus he recognised supreme authority—the kind of authority that didn't need to come and directly supervise a job to see that it was done, anymore than the emperor would directly supervise a repair work in an outlying province. Jesus, like the emperor, just needed to say the word.

In Matthew's account of this incident, it is followed later that evening by the storm on the lake where Jesus commanded the winds and waves to be still and then, the next day, the encounter with the man possessed by a collective of demons calling themselves 'Legion'.

All three of these events are connected by a single theme: that of authority in the legions. It may not be obvious that this is so regarding the tempest but it would not have escaped any early reader of the stories. A famous incident in the life of Julius Caesar was retold by many writers of antiquity.[186] Caesar, needing to find out why his troops were delayed in arriving at the front, had disguised himself as a slave and went aboard a twelve-oared boat. A storm blew up as the vessel attempted to pass over a river bar into the sea. The cross-currents were so dangerous that the captain decided to turn back before they all drowned. At the moment he gave this order, Caesar threw off his disguise and declared, 'Be

---

186 These writers included Dio Cassius, a Roman statesman and historian who wrote 80 volumes of history; Plutarch, the Greek biographer and essayist; Appian, a Greek historian; Suetonius, a Roman historian and biographer; Florus, a Roman historian; and Lucan, a Roman poet.

of good courage, men, knowing you carry Caesar and Caesar's fortune.' The captain ordered his rowers to redouble their efforts, but it was to no avail. Caesar had no authority over wind or water and eventually, defeated, they were forced to turn back.

Matthew's point in the three interlinked stories in his gospel was that Jesus had authority greater than that of Julius Caesar, the army commander who had been pronounced a god on his death. Augustus and Tiberius used the title *'son of a god'* in recognition of this deification. In the fourth gospel, John makes the same point in a different way:

> *Jesus answered him, 'You would have no authority over Me at all, if it had not been given to you from above; for this reason the one who handed Me over to you has the greater sin.'*
>
> John 19:11^{NASB}

Just as there are two kings at odds in the trial before Pilate—Jesus and Caesar—so there are two kings in the background of the royal official's story—Rehoboam and Jeroboam. We might also consider that, if the royal official is indeed Chuza, then the authority of Jesus and Herod is also being compared. In addition, we have an explanation why John was able to record the dialogue between the official and his servants when he met them on the way home.[187] Chuza told his wife who in turn told the story during her time travelling with Jesus. It wasn't just the son who was healed, so too was the wife.

Perhaps that too is part of the recapitulation of Jeroboam's history. Like Moses, Jeroboam was tasked with setting the people free from a tyrannical ruler—Solomon. Tragically, Scripture uses the same words to describe Solomon as were previously used for the

---

187 This information can only have come from the official himself or his servants.

Pharaoh of the Exodus. Both were cruel and oppressive leaders, treating the Hebrews as slaves in their building projects. And just as that Pharaoh tried to kill Moses, so Solomon tried to kill Jeroboam. And like Moses, he fled to a foreign country where he wed a foreign wife. In a bit of a twist, he went to Egypt—and then, again like Moses, when he left it seems that the old cliché came true: it's one thing to take a man out of Egypt, it's entirely another to take Egypt out of the man. On becoming king of ten of the tribes of Israel, Jeroboam set up rival sanctuaries to the Temple in Jerusalem—one at Bethel in the south, one at Dan in the north. In each place he erected a golden calf. To complete his connection with Moses, the priests who served at the shrine in Dan were the descendants of Jonathan, the grandson of Moses.

In the previous volume in this series, the mantle of Moses was discussed. Nicodemus received it from Jesus and was responsible for repairing the tear in it that resulted from Moses striking the rock to draw water, instead of speaking to it. Here we see one of the people who, in the long centuries between Moses and Nicodemus, was a carrier of that mantle. Jeroboam started well, just as Solomon started well. Jeroboam had been chosen by God to bring reform to the harsh subjugation of the people that marked Solomon's later years—but, through those golden calves, he became renowned for all succeeding centuries as the king who caused Israel to sin.

The prophet Ahijah's curse on his house was harsh and ominous. It must have broken the heart of Jeroboam's wife to hear a sentence of death pronounced on her son and doom on her family. Perhaps the age-old grief of a woman losing her child is a built-in part of this recapitulation of the death of Jeroboam's son.

Yet the reversal of Jeroboam's sin is evident in the way Chuza and Joanna honour Jesus and support His ministry. Their actions are a complete contrast with those of Jeroboam who turned others from God. Instead they provided the means for others to turn to God through their ministry support. Once again, the overturning of dispossession—as was so notable with the passing on of Joseph's mantle—is accomplished by a man and a woman working together.[188]

---

188 The dispossession that features so strongly in the Jeroboam story raises the question of whether he actually had Joseph's mantle—and whether that was, in fact, what enabled him to take such a huge piece of David's mantle. Further to this question, Jeroboam's wife was Shishak's sister-in-law, Ano. Jeroboam therefore had an Egyptian wife, just like Joseph. Ano as a Hebrew name would be derived from 'anah' and thus related to Anat, just like Joseph's wife Asenath. Jeroboam not only dispossessed the House of David, he also dispossessed the people by setting up golden calves and luring the people into idol worship. Those who carry Joseph's mantle are meant to facilitate the return of inheritance to the dispossessed, but when they operate it in unholy ways, they become dispossessors.

7.6 ABIJAH

THE PROPHET AHIJAH SAID OF the child Abijah, 'He was the only one in Jeroboam's house in whom the Lord God of Israel found anything good.'

Abijah means *my father is Yahweh*. Although we're apt to contrast Barabbas, *son of the father*, to Jesus, a much more fitting comparison is Abijah, the innocent son who pays the price for the nation turning its back on God under the leadership of his father. Abijah dies and is properly buried, mourned by all Israel.

If Abijah is a type of Jesus and his story is being recapitulated, then a restored plotline should involve a woman who is the counterpart to Jeroboam's wife and therefore witnesses Jesus' return from death. Such a woman is Joanna, wife of Chuza. Although she's only mentioned in Luke's gospel, her importance is signalled by her central placement in a chiastic structure.[189]

---

189   See: humbleskeptic.com/p/joanna-an-obscure-disciple-or-lukes (accessed 2 December 2024) I have actually slightly amended the chiasmus outlined at this site.

   A *When they came back from the tomb*

      B they told all these things to the Eleven[190] and to all the others.

         C *It was* MARY MAGDALENE

           D JOANNA

         C' MARY *the mother of James*

      B and the others with them who told this to the apostles…[191]

   A *Peter, however, got up and ran to the tomb.*

Joanna is sometimes thought to be the Hebrew name for the woman Paul describes as 'outstanding among the apostles'[192] who was, at some stage, in prison with him and who was also in Christ before he was. Her name, given by Paul as 'Junia', is a Latin form of Joanna. She is coupled with Andronicus in Paul's epistle—suggesting this is either Chuza's Greek alter ego, or the name of her second husband after widowhood, or her son's name.

Perhaps Junia and Joanna are not the same person; however, to be designated as 'outstanding amongst the apostles' means that she had to have:

- seen the Risen Lord
- gone above-and-beyond in following Jesus.

---

190 Are 'the Eleven' the same as the apostles in the mirror part of the chiasmus? Why would Luke repeat himself? *Did* he repeat himself? Is it possible 'the Eleven' is an entirely different group to the twelve apostles minus Judas as is traditionally thought? These questions will be examined in the next book in this series, *Bathing in Bronze*.

191 The verse *'But they did not believe the women, because their words seemed to them like nonsense'* briefly interrupts the chiasmus.

192 Romans 16:7[NIV]

There are very few women in that category. The only one we know of, other than Joanna, is Mary Magdalene. In Eastern Orthodox tradition, Junia and Andronicus went to the Roman province of Pannonia where they preached the Gospel with great success.

In Joanna we see devotion of the highest order. She was not only a major donor towards Jesus' ministry and one who travelled with Him, sitting at His feet as He taught His disciples—an unusual privilege for a woman in that era—but she was one of the women who encountered the angels in His tomb on the day of resurrection.[193]

In her we see who Jeroboam's wife was meant to be. Abijah was named for Yahweh so she obviously had at least minimal devotion to the Lord. However her husband's commitment to the golden calves defiled whatever belief she possessed. In Chuza and Joanna we see husband and wife working together[194] to support the advancement of the kingdom of God—precisely what Jeroboam and his wife were called to, almost a millennium previously.

---

193 Some rabbis of the period cursed those who allowed a woman to learn the Torah. Once again, we see a 'king mentality' that not only created an elite class and a slave class, but ensured that what the elite said could never be questioned.

194 Perhaps we also see a parallel and contrast to Deborah and Barak in this story of Jesus and the royal official. The official believed the word of the Lord as given to him and didn't have to have Jesus accompany him back to Capernaum, unlike Barak needing Deborah to come with him. Barak came from Kedesh in the tribal territory of Naphtali. Like Capernaum, Kedesh was on the western shore of the Sea of Galilee—so both Barak and the royal official are coming from the same general area. They are also going to the same general area and approximately the same distance—in Barak's case to Mount Tabor and in the official's case to Cana.

7.7 The Seventh Hour and Beyond

As he was going down, his servants met him and told him that his son was recovering. So he asked them the hour when he began to get better, and they said to him, 'Yesterday at the seventh hour the fever left him.' The father knew that was the hour when Jesus had said to him, 'Your son will live.' And he himself believed, and all his household. This was now the second sign that Jesus did when He had come from Judea to Galilee.

John 4:51–54[ESV]

From then on, Pilate tried to set Jesus free, but the Jewish leaders kept shouting, 'If you let this man go, you are no friend of Caesar. Anyone who claims to be a king opposes Caesar.'

John 19:12[NIV]

It's difficult to know whether John has reported the exact words of the servants of the royal official or if he's translating them for his audience. If we have the precise words, then 'the seventh hour' is one o'clock in the afternoon. But if they have been modified for the benefit of a mainly Gentile audience, and are reckoned according to Roman time. then 'the seventh hour' is seven o'clock in the morning.

At the sixth hour—which must be according to Roman time measurement in order to harmonise with the synoptic gospels—Pilate had proclaimed Jesus as king. It was therefore just after dawn. It was just after the sixth hour when the chief priests threatened Pilate, *'If you let this man go, you are no friend of Caesar. Anyone who claims to be a king opposes Caesar,'* culminating their dodgy argument—since, after all, there were many tribal kings[195] around the empire—with the shout, *'We have no king but Caesar.'*

With those words, they signed their own spiritual death warrant. God will not protect them when they decide, as happens within a generation, to shake off Caesar's rule.

By contrast, while the chief priests were choosing treason against God, a new dawn of faith was rising for the official. *'Your son will live,'* Jesus had said of the boy whose story was a recapitulation of Abijah, *my father is Yahweh*. Through the chiastic placement, John creates a subtle prophecy by Jesus, the Son of God, of His own return from the dead.

Once again, John reinforces belief as both the condition for salvation[196] and its result.

The timing of the meeting between the official and his servants depends on the system John is using and also if he's quoting the servants verbatim. It would take about eight hours to walk from Cana non-stop to Capernaum. So if the official met Jesus at seven in the morning, then he should be home by three in the afternoon or perhaps a few hours later if he stopped for rest and refreshment. However, since the servants say, *'Yesterday,'* this suggests the meeting is after midnight—at least by the Roman

---

195   Including, of course, a very local king in Herod Antipas. Perhaps, technically, they did not regard him as a king but as a 'tetrarch'.
196   In its wider sense, thus encompassing healing.

method of counting the hours. On the other hand, if the official set out at the seventh hour by Jewish reckoning—one o'clock in the afternoon—and didn't stop, he would make it home by nine that night. The moon would be not quite full but it would still be more than sufficient to light the path. But he didn't get the whole way before coming across his servants. In the Jewish system their, *'Yesterday,'* simply tells us this encounter occurred after sunset. That was the time the new day started. Sunset in Israel can be as early as 4:45 in winter and as late as 7:50 in summer. Assuming it's correct to date Jesus' stay with the Samaritans at the beginning of Tabernacles and the meeting with the royal official a few days later, then sunset at that time of year would be between 6:30 and 7:00 pm.

Sundown during Passover would also be around the same time. I am inclined to believe that John is quoting the precise words of the servants and that they are working according to a Jewish system of hours. The royal official would have been travelling—walking with rest breaks—for an absolute minimum of seventeen hours if this is the Roman system, but only six hours if it's the Jewish system.

Therefore the hour the 'little king' would have been on his way home and inquiring of his servants about the precise time of his son's recovery would have corresponded to the hour when the disciples of Jesus would have been returning home after interring Him in the tomb. Jesus is wrapped in myrrh and night at that moment.

The boy, however, has passed out of the shadow of death and into life.

7.8 The Second Sign

What does John mean when he uses the word *'sign'* in the statement:

> *This was now the second sign that Jesus did when He had come from Judea to Galilee.*
>
> John 4:54^{ESV}

What was the first sign? The only possibility, given that it had happened en route from Judea to Galilee, is the ingathering of the Samaritans to His fold. I discount the usual interpretation of the first sign as the wedding at Cana, because John comments that this happened *'when He had come from Judea to Galilee.'*

Now there are 17 references to signs in John's gospel.[197] Not all of these are references to miracles. Of the seven (or eight) sign-miracles recorded, only two are actually numbered. Both of these numbered signs occurred in Cana. Perhaps Cana is given this preferential treatment to emphasise the Joseph link in both the first and second signs: Jeroboam, after all, was descended from Joseph through Ephraim and, as noted in *The Summoning of*

---

[197] John 2:11, 2:18, 2:23, 3:2, 4:48, 4:54, 6:2, 6:14, 6:26, 6:30, 7:31, 9:16, 10:41, 11:47, 12:18, 12:37, 20:30. For detailed information on the significance of the number 17 as a reference to the most primitive form of Yahweh—'aahweh'—and thus an indication of the divinity of Jesus, see *The Elijah Tapestry*, the first book in this series. Yahweh means He Is who He Is, and *not* I Am who I Am. Rather it is Ehyeh that means I Am who I Am; and 'aahweh' is an archaic form of 'ehyeh'.

Time, the miracle at the wedding feast of Cana is about a symbolic reversal of the dispossession first set in motion by Joseph during the years of the famine in Egypt.

Now John is not simply using *sign* as an alternative word for *miracle*. His meaning must encompass *miracle* but not to replace it. Rather it must augment it. The Greek word for *sign* can also mean a *token* or a *distinguishing mark*. It is a symbol of authenticity, an emblem of corroboration or an insignia of confirmation. It endorses the person as genuinely who he says he is. He's the Saviour of the World, He's the Son of God, He's the Messiah, He's the Tehab, He's the King.

The Canaanite goddess Anat, the war-spirit who claimed the right to appoint the king of the gods, has not disappeared as an opponent in the story when Jesus left Sychar. One of the several possibilities for the meaning of her name is *sign*, as in 'an indication of Baal's will'. WF Albright equated 'Anath' with Hebrew "et', Aramaic "enet' and Akkadian 'ittu', *sign, time, destiny*.[198] As such, she would be a rival to Yahweh Nissi, *the Lord my banner* or *the Lord my sign*.[199]

Now there are several Hebrew words for a *sign*. One is 'oth', meaning a *token, mark* or *miracle* as well as *evidence to authenticate a message*. Another word for *sign* is 'chatham'. It also carries overtones of *authenticity* and likewise means a *mark*. However

---

198 Originally he suggested her name meant *providence*, then later *symbol* or *sign*. See: Ariella Deem, *The Goddess Anath and Some Biblical Hebrew Cruces*, academic.oup.com/jss/article-abstract/23/1/25/1640047 (accessed 10 September 2024) It should also be pointed out, however, that Anat is also virtually identical to the Canaanite word for *furrow*, thus linking her name back to the harvest Jesus pointed out at Sychar.

199 Yahweh Nissi links back into John's third chapter where Jesus talks about being lifted up from the earth. The particular Hebrew word for *banner* or *sign* here refers to things that are *raised* or *lifted on high*.

it also refers to a *seal*. When Tamar was negotiating with Judah, she asked for a guarantee he would send payment to her for her sexual services, requiring as surety his 'chatham', *seal*, plus his cord and his staff.[200] That *seal* or *sign* would have been attached to his mantle or else worn on a cord around the neck.

A sign authenticating Jesus' divinity could also be considered a seal and thus be attached to a mantle. The first sign at Shechem—the ingathering of the Samaritans and the return of their allegiance to the line of David—was connected in a spiritual sense to David's mantle; and so was the second sign. The Son of David did not reunite the pieces that had passed down from Rehoboam and Jeroboam—in an incredibly surprising move, He handed one to a Samaritan woman and one to a Nabataean man.

It seems, at first sight, as if Jesus is not returning the inheritance of the House of David to its rightful heirs but, in a revolution worthy of either Jeroboam or Barabbas, He's handing it over to outsiders.

What in heaven was He thinking? Why on earth would He create such an inconceivable upheaval?

When I first realised Jesus had handed David's mantle on to two people who were unnamed in Scripture, I simply couldn't believe it. The more research I did, the more it seemed likely that both of these unnamed people were foreigners. That was almost inconceivable. But I checked and rechecked the stories and their wordings, only to convince myself more firmly that Jesus had done the unthinkable and it really had happened. But why? What was the meaning behind the gift? Why those particular recipients? And what was the significance of their anonymity? And their outsider status?

---

200   Genesis 38:18

Here are my tentative thoughts:

- If Jesus had given the mantle to a Jewish man or woman, they would have automatically and instinctively thought of themselves as kings in the style of David.
- Yet there was *never* supposed to be a king in Israel. Therefore to give David's mantle to an Israelite would legitimise the very thing God had never approved, but only permitted. Yahweh alone was meant to be king. God doesn't call David 'king' when He's pointing out the fact the Temple is not something He ever asked for, but that it's completely David's idea: instead He calls him 'nagid' meaning *leader, prince, commander*.[201] David, it would therefore seem, should have refused the kingship and said to the people, 'There is only one king in Israel—the Lord Almighty. Thank you for the honour but let us return to the Lord's original plan for the rulership of the land. Please accept this alternative: I will be your champion as in the days of the judges.'
- But David didn't do that. He wanted to make a name for himself. That's why, in my view, the two inheritors of his mantle in the time of Jesus are anonymous. It's a statement about ambition and fame. The builders of Babel wanted to make a name for themselves too. So did Saul. In fact, Samuel told Saul that he'd lost the kingdom over prioritising building a memorial to himself rather than obeying God. Now the evidence for David's similar ambition has to be pieced together. It's not simply stated as a cut-and-dried fact in one single verse so that his aspirations are laid bare. The first clue that he wanted to

---

201 2 Samuel 7:8. Note that when Ezekiel prophesies about the building of the New Jerusalem, there is no specific provision for a king but rather for 'nasiy', *a prince, chief,* or *commander*. (Ezekiel 48:22)

make a name for himself is that, after killing Goliath, he took the giant's head to Jerusalem. This is extremely odd, because he'd have had to have hiked for at least five or six hours to do so. And, at the time, Jerusalem was a Jebusite fortress named Zion.[202] It was a Canaanite stronghold and it was about another 25 years before David would get around to conquering it. So the only possible reason for placing the head, as a sign, in front of the fortress is intimidation. It's like saying, 'You're next!' But why did David want Zion when no one from Joshua through to Saul had had the slightest interest in it? The next clue is given when Joab is attacking Rabbah of the Ammonites. He sends a message to David who is dallying in Jerusalem with Bathsheba:

> *I have fought against Rabbah and taken its water supply. Now muster the rest of the troops and besiege the city and capture it. Otherwise I will take the city, and it will be named after me.*
>
> 2 Samuel 12:27[NIV]

'Named after me.' Apparently, Joab knew what would give David incentive to come to battle. Also apparently, the only way it was possible a place could be named the 'City of David' was to take it from the Gentiles. That's why David wanted Jerusalem when no one else had ever given it a second glance. It's interesting to note that, in both narratives of David dancing before the Lord, the Ark of the Covenant is conspicuously brought to the 'City of David', rather than to Jerusalem or Zion.[203]

---

202 Zion means *dry, wasteland, parched*, or *desert*. When Isaiah prophesies that the Lord will comfort Zion (51:3), he is speaking of God rebuilding our wastelands.

203 The term 'City of David' is used 1 Chronicles 15:29 as well as three times in 2 Samuel 6:10–16 where David's entry with the Ark is described.

- David's mantle comes down the faithline from Abraham. And that means David was called to heal history with respect to the sins of Abraham and also to further advance Abraham's legacy. Let's compare the parallels in their lives:
    - David had a salt covenant with God; Abraham had blood, name, threshold and salt covenants.
    - David and Abraham were both prophets.
    - David's first capital was Hebron,[204] where Abraham had settled and was buried.
    - Both men warred as far as Damascus.
    - Each had a warband—Abraham's was 318 strong, David's was about 400.
    - David had a covenant with the Philistine king Achish (called 'Abimelech' in Psalm 34)[205] as Abraham did with the Philistine king of the same name in his own era.
    - David deceived Achish/Abimelech of Gath, and Abraham deceived Abimelech of Gerar.
    - Both David and Abraham believed their lives were under threat when they sought protection from their respective Abimelechs and both were prepared to sacrifice innocent strangers to save their own skin.

---

204 Apart from wanting a city named after him, David may have wanted to move from Hebron because it was a city of refuge. Although he completely disavowed Joab's action in acting as an avenger of blood and killing Abner, it probably occurred to him that Joab had a point about enemies turning up on your doorstep, claiming sanctuary and asking for covenant. Perhaps he wanted to avoid a similar scenario in the future and had already decided to look for a new capital before he conquered the fortress of Zion.

205 This psalm is quoted—in my view, far from coincidentally—in the section *adjacent to the chiasmus* for this scene in Samaria. Not perfect reflection, but close. 'Not one of His bones will be broken,' says John 19:36[NIV], referring to the fulfilment of the Scripture prophesied in Psalm 34:20[NIV], 'He protects all His bones, not one of them will be broken.'

Abraham knew that the previous time he'd asked his wife to say she was his sister, some Egyptians had died as a result of his dishonesty. He therefore was putting the people of Gerar in harm's way to save himself. David is clearly called to fix this aspect of Abraham's mantle but instead of mending it, he makes it worse. Abraham intended to sacrifice others; David actually does so by massacring whole cities to ensure Achish never discovers his duplicity.

- David put his wives and the family of his men in harm's way by leaving them alone, just as Abraham put his wife in harm's way by leaving her alone in Abimelech's harem as well as putting the families of Gerar in danger.

- David takes Uriah's wife into his harem; Abraham's wife is taken by Abimelech into his harem.

- Both men were given favour, rewards and resources by the Philistine king. Achish gave David the fortress of Ziklag which became part of Judah. Abimelech gave Abraham flocks, herd and slaves.

- David was passive in the face of abuse by his son and Abraham was passive in the face of abuse by his wife. They tolerated mistreatment and did not step up to deal with it.[206]

---

206   Abraham offered legal right to the spirit of abuse to test him by what he did at Gerar. He was willing to sacrifice others to save himself. He failed to trust God. Likewise, David offered legal right to the spirit of abuse by allowing human sacrifice. He was willing to sacrifice others to save himself from any possibility that the Gibeonites would refuse to bless the land. He thereby fell into their trap. They cursed the land instead, by allowing bodies to remain unburied. In addition, David was neglectful in relation to his wife, Michal. She obviously had idols (household gods, the same as the kind that Rachel stole from her father) which she used to hide David's escape. However David, unlike Jacob, apparently did nothing about them.

- ▷ David abandoned his daughter Tamar after she is raped; Abraham abandoned his second wife Hagar.
- ▷ David has nothing to do with Michal; Abraham expels Hagar.
- ▷ David hears an angel at threshing floor on Mount Moriah being told to stay his hand; Abraham is told by an angel at Mount Moriah to stay his hand.
- ▷ David declares his sons priests in the line of Melchizedek, while Abraham pays tithes to Melchizedek.

- Where Abraham got things wrong, David made them worse. Where Abraham got things right, David didn't. The mantle inherited from Abraham was so deeply defiled by David—yes, the man after God's own heart who, unfortunately, became much less so as time passed—that Jesus' response was apparently to *begin again*. To choose some kinsfolk of Abraham's whose ancestry went back to Ur of the Chaldees and start over. This is the most seriously damning indictment possible on the reign of David and the kings who followed him.
- The kingship of David is *nothing* like the kingship of Jesus. *Nothing*. Until we separate the two in our minds, we will always chase earthly power and mistake it for the glory that heaven offers. Our desire for heroes, both in Scripture and in our daily lives, creates leadership idols who cannot be questioned or doubted. Yet the very best are flawed—while nonetheless being God's instruments for good. The worst are manipulators of His kindness and mercy. David did not end well. He was not permitted to build the Temple because he'd shed so much blood—but his deathbed instructions to his son to dispose of a few people who'd aggravated him in life mean that Solomon's

reign starts in bloodshed and taints the Temple project right from the start.

- The kings of Israel were meant to be servant-kings. As Charles Ringma points out, servanthood translates power *over another* into power *for the other*.[207] The 'little king' who was nonetheless a royal official—a servant—and who, if I am correct in identifying him as Chuza supported Jesus' ministry financially and also allowed his wife to become an apostle, is the epitome of that principle of directing the power of kingship to serve *the other*.

---

[207] Charles Ringma, *Hear the Ancient Wisdom: A Meditational Reader for the Whole Year from the Early Church Fathers to the Pre-Reformation*, Cascade Books, 2013

7.9 The Divine Right of Kings

The Authorised Version of the Bible commissioned by King James was far from the first translation into English. Prior to it were various publications by John Wycliff, William Tyndale, Myles Coverdale, Thomas Matthew (John Rogers), a group of persecuted Anglicans who produced the Bishops' Bible and some English refugees who put together the Geneva Bible. The Matthew Bible was a completion of Tyndale's work and was the basis of the Great Bible.

When James VI of Scotland came to the throne of England as James I, he sponsored a new English translation. For centuries, it was the standard text. It is still beloved by many people. Part of James' motivation was, unfortunately, fleshly rather than godly. None of the previous translations gave a solid grounding for his theological leanings spelled out in his pamphlet, *The True Law of Free Monarchies*. There he expounded on the divine right of kings, seeing it as an extension of apostolic succession, and thus not subject to human law. James believed that, as an absolute monarch, he was above the will of the people and not accountable to any earthly authority.

Consequently, although the Geneva Bible was the most popular in England, it was ill-suited to James' way of thinking since it had translated the word *king* as *tyrant* about four hundred times. Notably, the word *tyrant* does not appear once in the King James

Version, presumably to make it less likely people would be critical of his monarchy.[208]

David's statement to God, 'Against You, You only, have I sinned,' is the epitome of a belief in the divine right of kings. David is asserting he is accountable to God, no one else. He is therefore not responsible to anyone for the harm they may have suffered as a result of his actions. Total submission is required, even when he is utterly wrong. When he decides on a census of the fighting men, Joab and his sub-commanders all ask David to rescind the order but he won't. Ten months go by and, in all that time, he doesn't realise he's defying God.[209] When he does recognise his sin and he's given three options regarding retribution, the people he's supposed to be shepherding pay the price. That's the usual outcome when leaders adopt a divine-right mentality and demand unquestioning obedience and unhesitating submission. In doing so, they insist on the level of loyalty and trust that should be given only to God.

---

208 The translators also faced the dilemma of rendering various Greek and Hebrew words for *deity* and *divinity*. Out of the many options available, they chose 'God' and 'Lord'. 'God' has the advantage of looking like it comes from *good*, although it actually derives from one of the titles of the Norse war-god Odin. 'Lord' on the other hand, while it looks and sounds natural to our eyes and ears because it's so familiar, might have been better translated as *king*. 'King Jesus' sounds strange, but it shouldn't. Bearing in mind that James believed in the Divine Right of Kings and that a *lord* is much further down the social hierarchy than a *king*, the choice is, in retrospect, a curious and provocative one.

209 1 Chronicles 21:1 says that the satan incited David to take a census. 2 Samuel 24:1 says it was God who incited David to do so. The two accounts are not mutually exclusive. As the first chapter of Job recounts, the satan asks permission to test Job but God takes responsibility for the outcome by later saying that the satan incited Him against Job. (Job 2:3) Thus it would appear from the two different accounts that the satan incited David to take a census because God gave permission for him to bring pressure to bear. This does not absolve David of surrendering to the pressure and therefore failing the test of trusting in God for the protection of the nation.

Back at the turn of the millennium, when the twentieth century was rolling into the twenty-first, a change took place in businesses across the world. Instead of *managers*, organisations started looking for *leaders*. A whole new range of criteria came to be expected: vision, innovation, inspiration, development, driving change, empowerment of people and an ability to mobilise them and draw the best out of them. This is the role of a prophet, but it's looked on as that of a king—and usually a king in the sense of an absolute monarch who carries the mandate of heaven.

Now, at the same time, in church circles, the notion of 'spiritual covering' came into vogue. A repackaging of the authoritarianism of the shepherding movement of the late twentieth century, it emphasised the blessings of obedience to leaders, even if they are wrong, and also stressed the curses that befall the families of those who are disobedient or noncompliant. It elevated church leaders to a religious throne and gave them spiritual licence for domination and coercive control. That leadership principle of 'empowerment of people' got smothered by 'covering'.

There are several words for *covering* in Scripture. The most significant of them is one that also means *atonement*. Can anyone be atonement for us, other than Jesus? Of course not. When David demanded that census take place, regardless of godly advice to the contrary—and I never cease to be amused by the irony of that godly advice coming from Joab[210] who strikes me as the least spiritually sensitive man in all Israel at the time—he

---

210 Joab actually found David's order to be so repulsive that he didn't actually count either the Levites or the men of Benjamin. That is a fascinating reaction—since the feud between Gibeah of Benjamin and Bethlehem of Judah was still ongoing at this point and Joab had had a major role in its continuation. Was Joab making a protest about David's action in allowing the Gibeonites to sacrifice the sons of Saul by refusing to add Saul's kinsfolk to the census tally? Was he protecting the smallest tribe against further decimation?

didn't need to do much to make it right. All David needed to do was pay an atonement tax. A census wasn't forbidden, so long as the lives of the warriors being counted were redeemed by a special payment.[211] But David didn't do what was needed—and as a result seventy thousand men died.

Obedience to David's command didn't 'cover' anyone. It didn't atone in any way. The demand of present-day leaders for submission and compliance in all circumstances, under the guise of offering their followers protective covering, is nothing short of a shield between believers and the atonement of Jesus. Some leaders even go further than 'protecting' their subordinates from the Lord's atonement—some use their authority to create double binds that have the horrific capacity to actually deny others access to the power of the atonement.[212]

Access to the atonement is right of entry to the benefits of salvation. Jesus, in redeeming us through the power of His atonement, didn't just win for us a home in heaven. With His blood, He purchased 'shalom' in all its variegated forms: *health, wholeness, completeness, soundness, welfare, prosperity*. Essential to 'shalom' is the making of amends, and the enactment of justice, restitution and recompense.

> Towards the end of World War II, General Eisenhower went to President Truman on hearing about plans to drop an atomic bomb on Japan and said that it was not the role of the military to be the conscience of the nation, it was to defend the country. He then argued against the plan on ethical grounds. Eisenhower's protest went unheeded. I imagine Joab would have recognised and sympathised with Eisenhower's dilemma. As commander of David's army, it was not Joab's role to be the conscience of Israel. But he was forced into the role by David's obstinate complicity with satanic powers.

211   Here's another time that David who confessed he *'loved the Law'*—the Law that, as king, he was supposed to regularly meditate on—either didn't know it or simply ignored it.

212   See: *Dealing with Rachab: Spirit of Wasting: Strategies for the Threshold #11*, Armour Books, 2025

Denial of access to the atonement is denial of access to 'shalom'.

Friends of mine had attended a very large church for thirty years. They'd invested enormous amounts of time and money in building it from a tiny congregation to thousands of Sunday worshippers. They were devastated when, not long after the church fired the pastor for being too 'pastoral' (no kidding!) and not enough like a forward-planning leader of vision and drive, they were asked to leave. They were too old for the youth-oriented church the new executive was planning. Although they resisted for a time, they were eventually pushed out.

A king had replaced a shepherd. It should have been no surprise when a high-profile fall involving abuse eventually occurred. The ancient desire for a king[213] like the nations has morphed today into a desire for a leader like the business world.

The Servant-Kingship of Jesus is not something that suddenly appeared in the gospels. It is evident in the stories of the patriarchs and prophets. There's no instant mindless obedience on their part when they are taken into God's counsel—so many of them immediately argue with Him, negotiating for mercy on behalf of the people.

---

213 The desire for someone to protect us in a crisis, to be a king-like leader, goes back much further than the era of Saul. We can see it even during the time of Moses when the people heard God announce the Ten Commandments: *'When the people saw the thunder and lightning and heard the trumpet and saw the mountain in smoke, they trembled with fear. They stayed at a distance and said to Moses, "Speak to us yourself and we will listen. But do not have God speak to us or we will die."'* (Exodus 20:18–19[NIV]) Already they have rejected direct communication with the Lord, wanting a leader to stand between them and God. They're already basically asking for a king other than God. They're looking for a mediator with the divine, forgetting that, as a kingdom of priests, they were meant to have direct access to God.

God made mankind in His image. But we've remade His image as the King, picturing Him in human terms—and instead of seeing favour and service, simply seeing tyranny. There is only one King with divine right—Jesus Himself.

7.10 Conclusion

David is the subject of so much praise throughout Scripture that we don't realise how much we are groomed by the adulation to believe that, one major lapse aside, he was the ideal king. We've been taught to view David by his achievements, thus allowing his foundational motivations to be concealed. We configure backwards from the Lord's promises to him—pledges that only have their fulfilment in Jesus—to think he must have deserved the rewards God showered on him, rather than realising that the mercy of the Lord prevailed.

We become what we hate. And David must have hated Saul immensely because he became so much like him. He broke all of his covenants with Saul and even with Jonathan. We tend to think the fact he didn't kill Saul when he had the opportunity means that he forgave him. But that's not necessarily the case. Forgiveness doesn't enter into the equation—it's all about avoiding a curse for violating covenant.

Unforgiveness sows poisonous seeds into our lives and from them spring bitter roots that defile many.[214] These roots grow to exhibit the same kind of behaviour in ourselves that we hate in others. So, David acted as a priest, just as Saul had done, and also like Saul,

---

214   Hebrews 12:15

David established a memorial in his own name. Saul's memorial is long-lost but David's was the city named after him.

The feud between Bethlehem and Gibeah could have been ended by David and, as we've seen, that could have been made possible by a child of the union of Michal and David. Their son on the throne would have removed so many of the tensions with the tribe of Benjamin and would have given Jerusalem as the capital a legitimacy it lacked while, century after century, a man of Judah ruled from outside the allotment of his own clans.

David's kingdom was, in every way, the absolute antithesis of the kingdom of heaven. It was the epitome of earthly power. It was a nation built on war, violence and bloodshed; a realm torn apart by a civil war precipitated by David's neglect, toleration of abuse and predatory sexual behaviour. It was a country under a curse because David wanted a blessing from the Gibeonites—yet, when they did the opposite, he simply ignored their defilement of the land and of God's Tabernacle.

Psalm 51 is David's song of contrition after he was confronted by Nathan regarding his affair with Bathsheba. Its fourth verse is stunningly narcissistic: *'Against You, You only, have I sinned…'*

It's basically saying that no one else's losses count. But, consider this: if David didn't sin against Uriah, or against the troops with Uriah who were slaughtered in the cover-up of his murder, or against the families of those soldiers, including their aged parents along with their widowed wives and orphaned children, or against Joab, Bathsheba, Bathsheba's family, the son she bore him and the nation itself, then how can we possibly suggest Absalom was treacherous? Or that Michal was wrong? Or that what Joab did was out of line?

If we only sin against God and not each other, then how can it matter what we do to one another? How is it that we're taught to overlook the rampant narcissism in what David wrote in that psalm? If I were to guess, the answer would simply be: because leaders, whether in the Christian world or outside it, want to be like David the giant-killer, the hero who *still* has a city-within-a-city named after him. In the secret recesses of our hearts, we worship David more than we worship Jesus. And so we're blinded to the egotism, the desire to be great in the earth, to have fame and fortune. Unable to look past David's own affirmations of his righteousness, and their repetitions by the chroniclers, we fail to see the carefully worded denunciations by the prophets. We therefore miss God's judgment on David in the temporal realm and overlook the fact it's the same as it was for Saul when it comes to similar actions.

Jesus is the touchstone through which we discern God's verdict on Abraham and David, Nehemiah and Ezra. It is only in Jesus that we can see the true meaning of His promise about an everlasting covenant. The anguished battering at the gate of heaven in Psalm 89 as it recites the covenant and then asks what happened should be sufficient clue that David's kingship was off-track, even at the start.

Jesus was the Servant-King, and He gave David's mantle of kingship not to the great and mighty of His age, but to two servants who would serve His kingdom. One lived in humble circumstances and one in a palace. Both were Gentiles—perhaps chosen because there was no chance they could ever dominate the Jews or set up a dynasty. The woman of Samaria, His cupbearer and kingmaker, served Him by becoming His first evangelist and reaping an instant harvest for Him. Chuza, the royal official, served as His financial supporter, as did his wife who became an apostle through her service at the resurrection.

In handing over a royal mantle to those who would be kingmakers, rather than kings, perhaps we see the fulfilment of Jacob's prophecy:

> *The sceptre will not depart from Judah, nor the staff from between his feet, until Shiloh comes and the allegiance of the nations is His.*
>
> Genesis 49:10[BSB]

Jesus, in giving away David's mantle at Shiloh, took the sceptre from the line of Judah and handed it to the influencers of His day, the servants who would uphold Him, not supplant Him.

It's significant He gave one part of the mantle to a woman and the other to a man. It tells us we're not to lord it over others—neither male over female nor female over male. This is about service, not supremacy.

Indeed David's mantle isn't so much about kingship as kingmaking. And Abraham's mantle was for the blessing of the nations. He had a revelation of Yahweh as the Most High God and King of the Universe but he kept it to himself. Both Abraham and David were called to be kingmakers. David's mantle and Abraham's mantle and, for that matter, Nehemiah's mantle are one and the same—and the assignment it carries is to lift up the name of the one true God so that He will be honoured as King forevermore. The task of those who inherit the mantle is to put a stop to the continual spiritual disenfranchisement of others by leaders who look to Abraham, David and Nehemiah as role models instead of to Jesus. They are appointed to introduce their community to the King so that each person has the opportunity to choose—or reject—covenantal allegiance and saving grace.

'The last shall be first,' Jesus said, 'and the first last.' Many of us haven't really believed Him. But at Sychar and Cana, He showed how seriously He meant that statement about the last becoming first. And in the chiastic parallel, John shows us the radical upside-down world where the Roman governor and the chief priests—the firsts of the nation—chose to be last.

In the inviolable kingdom, our role as kings is to be kingmakers—by crowning Jesus as Lord and offering Him dominion of our hearts and sovereignty of the wellspring of our lives. It's to cast our crowns before Him, to vacate the throne of self and surrender it to Jesus. It's to be leaders by being servants. Our role is also to be priests—to mediate God to others by introducing them to Jesus and His Kingdom.

We are to fulfil the same call that summoned Abraham out of Ur of the Chaldees and into the land God chose for His own: we are to carry Christ the Light into the dark world.

Other Books by Anne Hamilton

STRATEGIES FOR THE THRESHOLD series

Dealing with Python: Spirit of Constriction (with Arpana Dev Sangamithra)
Dealing with Ziz: Spirit of Forgetting
Name Covenant: Invitation to Friendship
Hidden in the Cleft: True and False Refuge
Dealing with Leviathan: Spirit of Retaliation
Dealing with Resheph: Spirit of Trouble (with Irenie Senior)
Dealing with Azazel: Spirit of Rejection
Dealing with Belial: Spirit of Abuse and Armies (with Janice Speirs)
Dealing with Kronos: Spirit of Time and Abuse (with Janice Speirs)
Dealing with Lilith: Spirit of Dispossession
Dealing with Rachab: Spirit of Wasting

DEVOTIONAL THEOLOGY series

God's Poetry: The Identity & Destiny Encoded in Your Name
God's Panoply: The Armour of God & the Kiss of Heaven
God's Pageantry: The Threshold Guardians & the Covenant Defender
God's Pottery: The Sea of Names & the Pierced Inheritance
God's Priority: World-Mending & Generational Testing
More Precious than Pearls (with Natalie Tensen)
As Resplendent as Rubies (with Natalie Tensen)
As Exceptional as Sapphires (with Donna Ho)
Spiritual Legal Rights (with Janice Sergison)
Core Values: Love (with Rebekah Robinson)
Core Values: Joy (with Rebekah Robinson)
Core Values: Peace (with Rebekah Robinson)
Core Values: Patience (with Rebekah Robinson)

JESUS AND THE HEALING OF HISTORY series

Like Wildflowers, Suddenly
Bent World, Bright Wings
Silk Shadows, Rings of Gold
Where His Feet Pass
The Singing Silence
In the Meshes of the Net
Interpreted by Love

Grace Drops with Anne podcast: https://gracedropswithanne.com

This series begins in Volume 1:

John 1 and 21: Mystery, Majesty and Mathematics in John's Gospel #1
ISBN 978-1-925380-53-8

The Elijah Tapestry is the first volume in an examination of the mirror-like chiastic patterning in the fourth gospel. John has designed his account of the life of Jesus as an epic poem in the style of Hebrew prophecy. This is demonstrated by aligning matching ideas at the beginning and end of the gospel.

As a result, a concealed theme is unveiled involving the passing of Elijah's mantle after the death of John the Baptiser. That legacy involves a divine assignment that has lain, dormant and unfinished, for nine centuries. Jesus, in reactivating the mantle, passes it to one of His disciples to carry on the work still to be fulfilled.

Volume 2:

John 2 and 20: Mystery, Majesty and Mathematics in John's Gospel #2
ISBN 978-1-925380-75-0

The Summoning of Time is the second volume in an examination of the mirror-like chiastic patterning in John's gospel. Once again, the match of parallel segments brings to light another hidden message that John embedded in his narrative.

There's a tendency to consider that a mantle is passed so the recipient can repeat the good works of the original owner—whereas, in John's gospel, it becomes clear it is passed so the unfinished works of the owner can be completed. In the first and last chapters, John addresses the matter of Elijah's mantle. In the second and second-last chapters, he turns to Joseph's coat-of-many-colours and shows us where Jesus bestowed it.

The wedding at Cana, the chasing of the money-lenders from the Temple and the meeting with Mary Magdalene in the garden are aligned in corresponding sections to reveal Jesus' message about the coming of a new era and the summoning of time.

Volume 3:

John 3 and 19: Mystery, Majesty and Mathematics in John's Gospel #3
ISBN 978-1-925380-67-5

The Lustral Waters is the third volume in the series, *Mystery, Majesty and Mathematics in John's Gospel*. One of the hidden themes in the symmetrical chiastic patterning of the fourth gospel is the passing of an ancient prophetic or governmental mantle from the keeping of Jesus on to various members of the family of faith.

In his third chapter, John features the legacy of Moses. He relies on his reader's knowledge of the extraordinary fame of Buni ben Gurion, nicknamed Nicodemus, 'Man of the Breakthrough', to augment his previous revelation about the summoning of time and also to unveil a critical understanding of what it means to be born from above.

This series continues in Volume 5:

John 5 and 18: Mystery, Majesty and Mathematics in John's Gospel #5
ISBN 978-1-923533-00-4

Bathing in Bronze is the fifth volume in a devotional-theology series that examines the poetic structure of John's gospel and brings to light hidden treasures buried in the front-to-back symmetry. In this book, the parallels between chapters 5 and 18 are explored.

What could the story of the man who was healed of a crippling condition at the Pool of Bethesda after 38 years of suffering possibly have in common with Peter's denial of Jesus in the courtyard of Caiaphas? The very last words of Socrates about owing a rooster to the healing god, Asclepius, provide us with an important clue.

www.ingramcontent.com/pod-product-compliance
Lightning Source LLC
Chambersburg PA
CBHW052017070526
44584CB00016B/1791